THE NEO-NAZIS
The Threat of the Hitler Cult

Also by Jerry Bornstein
Unions in Transition

With Sandy Bornstein
What Is Genetics?
New Frontiers in Genetics

THE NEO-NAZIS
The Threat of the Hitler Cult

Jerry Bornstein

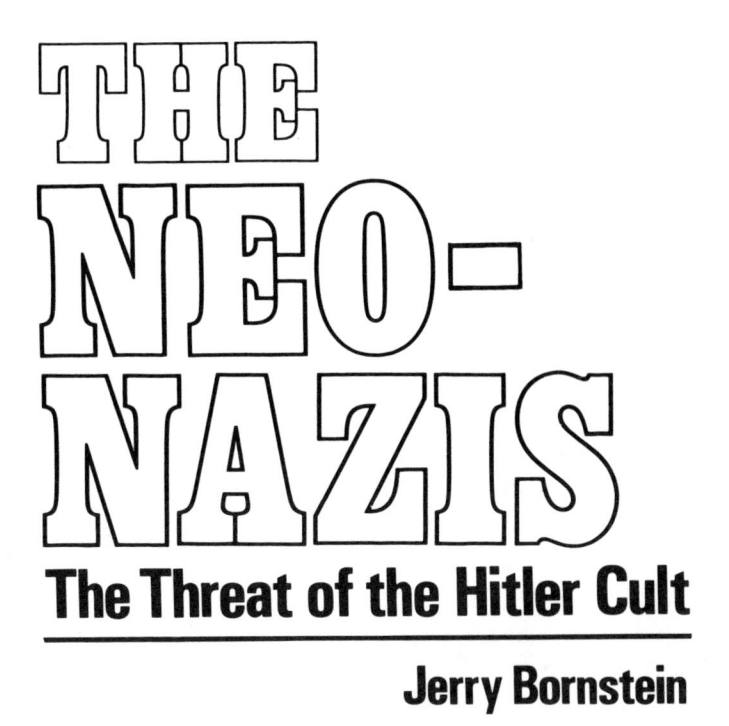

Julian Messner New York
A Division of Simon & Schuster, Inc.

Copyright © 1986 by Jerry Bornstein
All rights reserved including the right to reproduction in whole or in part in any form. Published by Julian Messner, A Division of Simon & Schuster, Inc. Simon & Schuster Building, Rockefeller Center, 1230 Avenue of the Americas, New York, New York 10020. Julian Messner and colophon are trademarks of Simon & Schuster, Inc. Photos: AP/Wide World. Manufactured in the United States of America. Design by Meredith Dunham.

10 9 8 7 6 5 4 3 2 1

Library of Congress Cataloging in Publication Data

Bornstein, Jerry.   Neo-Nazis.
  Bibliography: p.   Includes index.   Summary: Observes the development of nazism in the United States from Hitler's time to today, the current status of Nazi followers, the psychology of the movement, civil liberties issues, and possible solutions. 1. Fascism—United States—History—Juvenile literature. 2. United States—Race relations—Juvenile literature. [1. Fascism—United States—History] I. Title.   E743.5.B65   1986   324.273'38   86-5363
ISBN: 0-671-50238-7

IN MEMORY OF
BENJAMIN BORNSTEIN,
MY GRANDFATHER

ACKNOWLEDGMENTS

Special thanks are due to Cyma M. Horowitz, Library Director of the American Jewish Committee's Blaustein Library, and to Jerome Bakst, Research Director of the Anti-Defamation League, for their assistance and cooperation in researching this book.

CONTENTS

Introduction 9

1 The Origins of Nazism 11
2 Nazism Comes to America 22
3 Purifying the Nazi Myth 42
4 Rockwell and the American Nazi Party 55
5 Splinter Groups and Kindred Organizations 68
6 Neo-Nazis and Electoral Politics 93
7 Neo-Nazism Around the World 98
8 International Links and Propaganda 114
9 The Nazi Personality 123
10 Free Speech for Nazis? 133
11 The Threat of Nazism Today 145

Bibliography 151
Index 155

INTRODUCTION

This is not a pleasant book. But it is a necessary book. It is a book about people who hate. It is about people who idolize the most despicable human being who lived in the twentieth century, perhaps in the entire history of mankind—Adolf Hitler. Some people actually believe that Adolf Hitler was the greatest man who ever lived. Their only regret is that Hitler's plan for a new order for world society did not succeed. These people are called neo-Nazis—members of a tiny movement, on the extreme fringes of political life, with a tremendous potential for violence.

It was not pleasant to do research about these neo-Nazis, to read their newspapers and their leaflets, knowing that their solution to all social problems facing society today is to kill people with Jewish-sounding last names like mine. After living through the civil rights struggles of the 1960s and prizing so highly the principles of brotherhood, I did not find it pleasant to read their racist categorizations of blacks as subhumans. It was not easy to read the filth and venom, lies and distortions that the neo-Nazis cherish as sacred principles, but which fly in the face of the principles I believe in and have tried to instill in my children.

The world thought it had destroyed Nazism during World War II. But it did not. The neo-Nazis may be politically insignificant today, but for some irrational reason, they exist. Their existence must be acknowledged and understood in its context. The potential danger these groups present to society must be examined. What is Nazism? What is its appeal? What are the neo-Nazi groups? What are their activities? What causes people to become Nazis? How does a democratic society adapt to the existence of such perverse political ideas in its midst? What dangers does this movement pose? You cannot deal with a social problem without trying to understand it first. Maybe someday we can have a world where hate groups no longer exist. But that day has not yet arrived.

JERRY BORNSTEIN

1
THE ORIGINS OF NAZISM

Nazism was an extreme right-wing movement that arose in Germany shortly after World War I. Fourteen years later the Nazis took power in Germany and plunged humanity into the most terrible war in world history. The movement derived its name from the Nationalsozialistische Deutsche Arbeiterpartei (NSDAP). In English, this means the National Socialist German Workers Party—or the Nazi Party, as it was called. Despite its name, however, the Nazi Party was not socialist, nor did it have the interests of the working classes at heart. Its use of the word "socialist" was merely a cynical attempt to gain mass acceptance by reflecting a lower-middle-class bias against big capitalists.

Nazism was a type of fascism, a form of government that confines power to a small minority led by a dictator. He wields absolute power and maintains order and discipline in society through a complete, or total, control of all major social institutions. Totalitarian is another name for this kind of government. The tentacles of the fascist state bureaucracy reach into every aspect of civil life. The government controls the media, suppresses civil liberties, quashes the freedom of labor unions, and limits the activities of social and political organizations. The government also enforces a rigorous discipline on the working classes, for the benefit of the state. Because the Stalinist regimes of Eastern Europe employ many of the same totalitarian techniques, there is an obvious similarity in the way the two systems rule. But the communist governments employ an ideology based on radicalism of the left. They champion the weak against the strong, promise social equality—which they don't deliver once in power—and oppose capitalism, usually taking over private industry outright.

Fascists, on the other hand, base their ideology on inequality, glorifying the strong and exploiting the weak. While fascist governments employ anti-capitalist propaganda, particularly in their early stages, they do so for the benefit of small-business owners who can't compete with big business or cannot continue to exist in a technologically changing world. They do not act in behalf of the workers. Once in power, fascists usually tone down their anti-capitalist rhetoric and try to accommodate big business interests—all the while insisting that business subordinate its interests to the militaristic needs and absolute power of the state.

The fascist state maintains the loyalty of the masses through its absolute control of the mass media and by whipping up nationalism and promoting a dream of militaristic greatness for the na-

The Origins of Nazism

Mussolini addressing a crowd of 60,000 people in Florence, Italy, in May 1930.

tion. The government emphasizes the superiority of the fascist nation over other countries, and it promises expansion and fulfillment of the nation's historic destiny. At the same time fascism fosters a garrison-state mentality, viewing outsiders and dissenters as enemies of the state and society. Fascist leaders use police-state tactics, such as brutal suppression and spying, to enforce political uniformity. These were the fundamental qualities of the fascism that developed in Italy and elsewhere after World War I. Nazism gave the world a peculiarly German form of fascism.

The founder and father of Nazism was Adolf Hitler. During World War I, Hitler was an obscure

THE NEO-NAZIS

non-commissioned officer in the German army. Like many other Germans, Hitler was infuriated by the defeat of the imperial army and the thwarting of German aims for expansion in Europe and in the colonies. And like many other right-wing Germans, the young Hitler blamed defeat on the rebellion of the German working class on the home front. This rebellion, led by socialists and communists, toppled the power of the Kaiser and caused the war effort to collapse. Hitler and others believed that the German army was defeated not on the battlefield by its enemies, but at home by German workers who acted treasonously.

The trench fighting of the First World War brought great loss of life and desolation to the countries of Europe.

The Origins of Nazism

The Weimar Republic, established after the fall of the Kaiser, ruled Germany until the Nazi consolidation of power in 1933. Those years were an uncertain period for Germany. The whole world seemed turned upside down. Germany had suffered national humiliation not only in the war but also in the harsh peace imposed by the victorious Allies under the provisions of the Treaty of Versailles. Nearly two million Germans had died in the fighting. Four million had been wounded and mutilated. Traditional German militarism was banned by the treaty. The economy was in shambles—destroyed by rampant inflation, the seizure of key industrial zones by France, widespread unemployment, and the collapse of the German people's confidence and hope.

Traditional values seemed to have disappeared. The future seemed hopeless. The power of the communists and socialists grew among the working class. Right-wing thugs and leftists clashed in the streets.

Workers struck and organized workers' councils modeled on the Soviets in Russia. Right-wing army veterans organized themselves into quasi-military groups called *freikorps,* and clashed in the streets with leftists.

In the midst of this upheaval, Adolf Hitler helped organize the Nazi Party in 1921. At this point it was just one of many right-wing militant groups that attacked the left and dreamed of restoring Germany to military greatness. Only later would the Nazis absorb the other groups. In 1923, Hitler led a band of followers in Munich in an abortive upris-

THE NEO-NAZIS

Inflation in Germany in the 1920s forced companies to use wheelbarrows to carry their weekly payroll, as seen here in Berlin in 1923.

ing, or *putsch,* which was immediately quelled. As a result, Hitler was sentenced to a term in prison, and his followers dispersed for the moment. But far from destroying the movement, Hitler's imprisonment in the long run strengthened it. It gave Hitler time to collaborate with a close comrade, Rudolf Hess, in writing *Mein Kampf* [My Struggle], a book that set forth the ideological basis for Nazism and became the bible of the movement.

Hitler drew heavily on the writings of earlier theorists in the right-wing German tradition. The roots of the full-blown Nazi ideology can be traced

The Origins of Nazism

back to the traditions of Prussian militarism and the spiritual inspiration of great soldiers and great leaders. Hitler also drew on certain German writers who opposed the values of democracy and egalitarianism that emerged from the French Revolution. Instead, they emphasized instinct, past traditions, and the power of the strong.

Another important intellectual movement that contributed to Hitler's theories was Social Darwinism, which applied Darwin's theories of evolution in nature to the development of human society. The concept of the *survival of the fittest* explains how nature permits the survival of the fittest individuals, so that their biological traits of strength or adaptability are passed on from generation to generation.

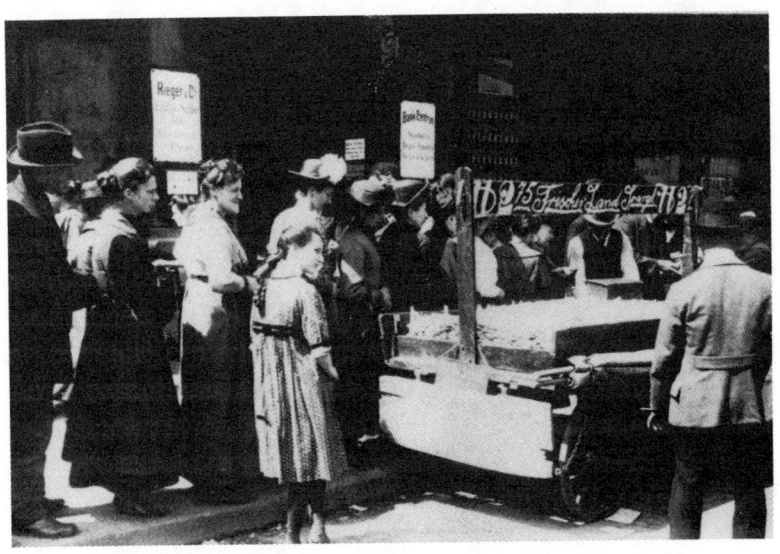

Inflation drove up the price of vegetables to the equivalent of $2.79 a pound in Berlin in the 1920s.

When this scientific concept was applied to human social problems it led to a rejection of sympathy, charity, and compassion for the poor and unfortunate. Social Darwinists had contempt for the poor, who were seen as inferior and therefore unfit for survival. This attitude led to a glorification of power, strength, ruthlessness, and even brute force. Indeed, Hitler saw an "eternal struggle" in society mediated only by brute force.

Hitler contributed intense racism and national chauvinism to this Social Darwinist tradition. The Marxists, on the left, saw history as a struggle between *classes*. Hitler, on the right, regarded history as a struggle between *races*. He believed the so-

Adolf Hitler addressing a rally of 1,500,000 Germans outside Berlin on May 1, 1935.

The Origins of Nazism

called Aryan race—the Germanic peoples—was superior to all others and was destined to rule the world. Hitler knew that the goal of ruling the world would not be easily attained and would require the complete mobilization of the German people in an unswerving loyalty behind the state. He designed a campaign of mass manipulation, relying on propaganda techniques and lies that he hoped would enable the Nazi movement to accomplish this goal. The key technique was to focus people's attention on a single enemy, an easily identifiable adversary that stood in the way of the Aryan race's fulfillment of its destiny.

Hitler wrote the following in *Mein Kampf*:

> The art of truly great popular leaders in all ages has consisted chiefly in not distracting the attention of the people, but concentrating always on a single adversary. The more unified the object of the people's will to fight, the greater will be the magnetic attraction of the movement and the more tremendous its impact. It is part of a great leader's genius to make even widely separated adversaries appear as if they belonged to one category....

Hitler chose the Jews as this single adversary. He genuinely hated Jews, and he seized the opportunity to use that hatred for political purposes. The Jews became for him the historic scapegoat, the personification of all that was "evil" in the world—communism, democracy, liberalism, social change, Moscow, and Washington.

Anti-Semitism had strong roots in Europe, going back generations, and it was easy to revive the peo-

THE NEO-NAZIS

Hitler addressing a crowd of 100,000 Nazi storm troopers at Nuremberg in September 1936.

ple's historical hatred and use it for new purposes. It was also important to attack Judaism, for the Judeo-Christian tradition of equality, justice, and charity was the antithesis of the Nazi ideal of the super race and social inequality. To attack the Christian church directly would not have been expedient, however, so Hitler chose to persecute only Jews. During his rule, anti-Semitism, a social problem that had scarred the life of Europe for centuries, was raised to the level of a science. Anti-Semitism, racism, and nationalism became the fundamental principles of Nazi thinking, and the ideological basis for military invasion and genocide.

The Origins of Nazism

In *Mein Kampf,* Hitler summed up his theory of hatred in these words:

> As often in history, Germany is the great pivot in the mighty struggle. If our people and our state become the victim of these bloodthirsty and avaricious Jewish tyrants of nations, the whole earth will sink into the snares of this octopus: if Germany frees herself from this embrace, this greatest of dangers to nations may be regarded as broken for the whole world.

The circumstances of Hitler's rise to power in Germany have been analyzed and debated by many historians and political analysts. Some have said that the economic ruins of a defeated Germany and the social dislocation of the middle classes laid the groundwork for Nazism's popularity. These social and economic problems were made worse by the onset of the Great Depression, which further increased the appeal of Nazism in the early thirties. Other historians cite the fear of communism, which led Hitler to strike an arrangement with leading German industrialists who believed they could save capitalism, prevent communism, and control Hitler for their own purposes. The appeal of Nazism to large numbers of middle-class Germans is something we shall return to in a later chapter.

2
NAZISM COMES TO AMERICA

Nazism existed in America long before Hitler rose to international notoriety. From 1924 to 1941, when the United States entered World War II following the Japanese attack on Pearl Harbor, the Nazi movement in America went through several distinct organizational forms. It began with the formation of a small cell of Nazi activists in the Bronx, New York.

Eventually the Nazi cell grew to a movement that comprised perhaps as many as 25,000 members, published newspapers, ran summer camps for children, distributed millions of pieces of propaganda, and managed to attract over 20,000 people to a rally in the old Madison Square Garden in New York City in 1939. The Nazis never succeeded in attracting a significant number of second-generation or naturalized German-Americans to their movement, however. Some 90 percent of their members were recent German immigrants who had arrived in this country in the decade following World War I.

Nazism Comes to America

Uniformed members of a German-American Bund color guard marching into Madison Square Garden in New York City for a rally in February 1939.

These immigrants shared the same anguish and frustrations as Hitler's followers in Germany itself.

As we have seen, Germany was in chaos. The Old World seemed to be dying, but a new one to replace it had not yet been born. The old crafts were dying out with the dawn of assembly-line technology. Many of the displaced craftsmen sought to escape.

During the period from 1919 to 1933, more than 400,000 Germans emigrated to the United States. They were very different from the 5 million German immigrants who had come earlier. They were socially and pyschologically scarred by the desperate situation at home. They were voluntary exiles from a defeated nation, bitter and disillusioned. They did not come to the New World looking for a better future. They were running away from a world of failure, looking for temporary refuge and dreaming of a day when they could return home to a powerful and prosperous Germany. Some were right-wingers who had fought in the streets of Germany against the leftists. Some were Nazis.

In 1922 a small group of expatriate Germans formed the first American Nazi cell in the Bronx. In the next two years they were joined by others, including some former German Nazi Party members. A national organization, the Nationalsozialistische Vereinigung Teutonia—the Teutonia Association—was founded on October 12, 1924, in Detroit. Its leaders included Friedrich Fritz Gissibl, who, upon his return to Germany later in the 1930s, was responsible for Nazi exiles returning from America. He was charged with integrating them into Nazi activities in Germany. Another founder was Josef Schuster, the only Nazi in the American movement who participated with Hitler in the Munich *putsch* in 1923 before fleeing to America.

By 1932 the Teutonia Association claimed to have branches in major cities including Detroit, Los Angeles, New York, Cincinnati, and Chicago. Most of the organization's five hundred members were merely Nazi sympathizers, not actual party members. The Teutonia Association published a newspaper extolling Hitler and his philosophy, and denouncing communism and Jews.

Unlike future Nazi organizations, the Teutonia Association did not undertake to convert the established German-American community to Nazism. Most members regarded themselves as exiles, temporarily in America, eager to return to Germany when conditions improved, and consequently their paper was aimed at other recent immigrants. The organization raised funds for the Nazi Party in Germany, and one of their proudest trophies was a personal thank-you note received from Hitler himself in 1926.

The Teutonia Association had a particularly strong branch in Detroit, with a number of members employed in the auto industry. This led some observers to speculate that Henry Ford, head of the Ford Motor Company, was a sympathizer of and contributor to the Teutonia Association, but this has never been proven conclusively. The charge is based on circumstantial evidence. Ford was a known anti-Semite. He had arranged for the publication in the *Dearborn Independent* of "The Protocols of Elders of Zion," a fraudulent anti-Semitic document. Because of his anti-Semitic reputation, Ford was approached in 1924 for financial support by an official of the German Nazi Party. Ford refused to make a contribution. A number of Teutonia Association activists were employees of the Ford Motor Company in Detroit, including Fritz Kuhn, the self-styled American führer of the Nazis who came to prominence in the late thirties.

Not all Nazis living in the United States were members of the Teutonia Association. About two hundred Nazi exiles organized Gauleitung USA, or

THE NEO-NAZIS

Fritz Kuhn, by radio from Detroit in 1937, denied that his German-American Bund had any connection with the German government.

Gau-USA, as it was called, which reported directly to the Nazi Party apparatus in Germany from 1931 to 1933.

Eventually the Teutonia Association and Gau-USA began feuding over who would be the official representative of the Nazi movement in the United States. The bickering led to resignations and undercut the potential impact of the movement in the German-American community at large. A handful of prominent pro-Nazi German-Americans complained to the party leaders that the infighting among the Nazis in America was harmful to the movement. Eventually the German officials ordered both organizations to disband in order to permit the formation of a mass-based pro-Nazi organization in America.

NAZISM IN AMERICA FLEXES ITS MUSCLES: THE ERA OF THE BUNDS

Following the seizure of power by the Nazis in 1933 the issue of party organization in foreign countries assumed a new significance for the Hitlerites. It was no longer a question of simply maintaining the loyalty of a few party adherents overseas. The activities of overseas party members now became an integral part of the German Reich's foreign policy and expansionist plans. The Nazi Party had not yet consolidated its control over the Foreign Ministry of the German government, particularly the career foreign service, which tended to have a much more traditional view of how diplomacy should be conducted than did the Nazis. The overseas party organization permitted the Nazis to undertake direct action in foreign countries. Overseas operations were not limited to America, but included countries ranging from Brazil and Argentina to Mexico, China, South Africa, Japan, Switzerland, and any other nation with a sizable German population.

The Nazi attempt to penetrate overseas German colonies was based on a theory that was later proved to be entirely false. As we have seen, the Nazis believed that race superseded nationality in importance. It didn't matter if German emigrants had become citizens of another country; they were still of German, or Aryan, "racial stock." Many party agencies were involved in the efforts to spread Nazism to Germans abroad. Academicians worked in institutes tabulating data and reanalyzing the history of German emigration abroad to provide tactical suggestions to make this work more effective and efficient.

The Nazis were particularly interested in the German-Americans in the United States, because there were so many of them and because of the military and industrial importance of the United States. Having a strong pro-German sentiment in the United States to undercut pro-Western democratic sympathies would be crucial in the years ahead, as German expansionism began in Europe.

The Nazis completely discounted the "melting pot" theory of the integration of foreign immigrants into American society. This theory held that a unique society was developing in the United States in which the contributions of a multitude of immigrant nationalities combined to enrich American culture as those immigrants became integrated into American society, while maintaining their own identity and traditions. The Nazis dismissed the melting pot theory as a "Jewish invention." Party academicians pointed out that an estimated six to seven million German-Americans still spoke German as their first language, and English only as a second language. They also noted that 25 percent of the American population in 1930 could trace its ancestry back to Germany.

In Hitler's view, the American nation was "Jew

infested" and "communist dominated," but he believed that the presence of so many "Aryans" meant that America had a "German backbone," which could restore American society to greatness under Nazism. Hitler believed that the turning point in American history was the Civil War in which the "beginnings of a great new social order based on the principle of slavery and inequality was destroyed." Hitler regretted the victory for the "falsities of liberty and equality."

The concept of *Deutschtum*—of Germanness prevailing over state allegiance—meant that it was possible to mobilize the German-American population behind a militant, dynamic German state—the Nazi state—which would make all Germans everywhere proud to be German, and turn them into a potent political force.

It wasn't long before this strategy was put into action in an aggressive manner in the United States. In 1933, Heinz Spanknobel, a member of both the Gau-USA and the Teutonia Association, traveled to Germany and met with Rudolf Hess. Impressed by Spanknobel's boisterous claims of pro-Nazi feelings in the United States, Hess gave Spanknobel authorization to set up a new Nazi organization in the United States. It would include both German nationals and German-Americans and be under the clandestine control of the Nazis.

The new organization, the Bund der Freunde des Neuven Deutschland (Friends of the New Germany), held its founding convention in Chicago on July 28, 1933, declaring as its goal the unification of all Germans who had immigrated to America in the preceding two hundred years. Spanknobel took the title of Bundesleiter. One of his first actions was to organize a strong, centralized fighting group, modeled after the storm troopers in Germany. Leadership of these thugs fell to Josef Schuster, the old Nazi street fighter who had been with Hitler at the Munich *putsch* in 1923.

Spanknobel took to his new leadership position with enthusiasm. He soon seemed to forget that he was in the United States, not Germany. He adopted an authoritarian style, which alienated more people than it attracted to the Nazi cause. Carrying a document from Rudolf Hess, which authorized him to

Heinz Spanknobel speaking at the opening of Nazi Party headquarters in New York City in 1932.

be the official representative of the Nazi Party in America, Spanknobel barged into the offices of a German-American newspaper in New York City and ordered the editors to publish articles favorable to Germany and Hitler. The editor and publishers of the newspaper threw the intruder out and made it their business to oppose his attempts to take control of the United German Societies in New York.

The United German Societies was an umbrella organization encompassing hundreds of German-American organizations in the New York City area. In September 1933 the UGS was hard at work planning festivities to mark German Day, the 250th anniversary of the first German migration to America. Accompanied by a band of his storm troopers, Spanknobel marched into a UGS planning session on September 18 and demanded the ouster of German-Jewish organizations that were members of the umbrella organization. Storm troopers threatened violence against any who disagreed. Representatives from four German-Jewish organizations withdrew.

Spanknobel then successfully insisted on being elected to the executive board of the UGS, and on inviting the German ambassador to address the October 29 German Day ceremonies. The Nazi leader failed, however, to win passage of a resolution to fly the German swastika flag over the building in which the ceremonies were to be held—a U.S. armory in Manhattan. The incident provoked considerable controversy in the German-American community. The German Day festivities were intended as a celebration of the German migration to

THE NEO-NAZIS

America and as an acknowledgment of the contributions German-Americans had made to their adopted homeland. Many were alarmed at the Nazi strong-arm attempt to take over the UGS and turn German Day into an open endorsement of the Nazi government of Adolf Hitler. Six more Jewish organizations withdrew from the UGS, and the entire executive board—with the exception of Spanknobel—resigned in protest. At a meeting of a reconstituted board, which he controlled, Spanknobel pushed through his proposal to fly the swastika.

The public uproar now spread to the New York community at large. Following a night of vandalism in which swastikas were painted on synagogue doors, New York City Mayor John Patrick O'Brien demanded a meeting with Spanknobel and other UGS board members to discuss possible cancellation of the celebration. Jewish organizations and liberal politicians went even further, demanding that Spanknobel be arrested and deported as an agent of a foreign government. Spanknobel, realizing the situation was out of control, went into hiding and fled the country, returning to Germany. The Spanknobel Affair, as it came to be known, was not an auspicious beginning for the Nazi movement the Germans wanted to build in America. Instead of enhancing the image of Nazism in the United States, it fortified the media's portrayal of the Nazis as thugs and misfits.

On orders from Germany, the next leaders of the Nazi movement, Ignatz Griebl and Hubert Schnurch, took a more low-key approach, emphasizing German cultural programs, believing this

Nazism Comes to America

would have a wider appeal in the United States. Naturally, the organization kept up its steady barrage of anti-Semitic propaganda, claiming that Jews were responsible for all the problems in the world. Jews were said to be motivated by greed and lust. The organization also published anti-black propaganda, claiming that blacks were dupes of the Jews and susceptible to communism. By 1934, the movement had stabilized with a membership of around five thousand.

Germany was less than pleased with the work in America. The overwhelming majority of German-Americans were loath to make the Nazi cause their own. The anticipated mass conversion of German-Americans to the Nazi movement never materialized. Many Nazi activities in the United States in the long run turned out to be embarrassing setbacks that repelled many German-Americans and caused a deterioration of both support and tolerance for the Nazi regime among Americans in general.

The U.S. government complained not only about human rights violations in Nazi Germany but frequently about the flamboyant antics of Nazis in the United States and subversion in other countries in the Western Hemisphere. Relations between the two nations became strained. Germany had hoped to use a massive Nazi movement in America to neutralize the United States in the conflict it was preparing for in Europe. However, Nazi activities in this country lent themselves to sensational press coverage that only increased antagonism toward the German Reich.

THE NEO-NAZIS

For political reasons, Germany decided to play down party organization in America and instead began a clandestine effort to stir up anti-Semitism in America. The Germans hoped to get better results by relying on indigenous American fascist organizations that had sprung up as the Great Depression wore on. These American groups included C. F. Fullerton's White Shirts and William Dudley Pelly's Silver Shirts. Nazi Germany became the chief supplier of political literature to these organizations.

Concluding that the Bund had become more of a burden than it was worth, the Nazi Party in Germany ordered all German citizens to resign from the Bund by January 1, 1936. Since German Nazi Party members constituted the nucleus of the Bund, it was assumed that this order would result in the disintegration of the organization. The German Nazis had miscalculated, seriously underestimating how well the newest Bund leader, Fritz Kuhn, had succeeded in implanting the organization among recent German immigrants. Far from disappearing, the Bund was just about to enter its brief golden era.

Fritz Kuhn was the strongest leader of the American Nazis. He changed the name of the organization to Amerika Deutschlander Bund, or German-American Bund, and declared himself the American führer. Kuhn's background was similar to that of other early Nazi activitists. Born in Munich in 1896, he fought in the German army during World War I. After the war, he joined the *freikorps* and brawled in the streets against socialists and communists. In 1921 he enrolled in the Nazi Party. In 1923 he moved to Mexico and found employment as a chemist. Later he immigrated to the United States. He joined the Bund comparatively late, in 1933. He became an American citizen in 1934 and was thus able to circumvent the party

Fritz Kuhn addressing a crowd at a bund camp near Andover, New Jersey, in May 1938.

THE NEO-NAZIS

Boys from Buffalo, New York, and Philadelphia drilling in a bund camp in New Jersey in August 1934.

order for all German nationals to cease active membership in the Bund. In March 1936 he took control of the organization.

Kuhn wanted to give Germans living in America the vicarious thrill of "experiencing" Nazism as practiced in Germany. He relied on ritual, uniforms, and ceremonies to stir up enthusiasm and emotions. He organized rallies and torchlight parades, and delivered demogogic speeches patterned after those given by the real führer in Germany. Denied continued financial support from Germany, Kuhn made the organization economically self-sustaining through the sale of literature, uniforms, and Nazi paraphernalia.

Nazism Comes to America

Under Kuhn's leadership the Bund gave heavy emphasis to indoctrinating young people. Youngsters were sent away to youth camps modeled after those run for the Hitler Youth in Germany. Young children dressed in brown uniforms. Young adults wore Nazi uniforms and sang songs extolling Nazism and Hitler. One song ended with these words pledging blind loyalty to the führer:

> Youth, youth, we are the future soldiers.
> Youth, youth, we are the ones to carry out
> future deeds.
> Führer, we belong to you; yes, we comrades
> belong to you.

Most historians believe that membership in the Bund may have reached twenty thousand at its high point. Relying on Hitler's "big lie" theory (that the masses will more readily believe a big lie than a small one), Kuhn made an inflated claim of a hundred thousand members. All the while this burgeoning growth was taking place, however, Germany was pulling back from the Bund. The American group's activities continued to damage German interests in the United States. Contact between the Bund and the German government was limited to low-level officials at the German consulate, and only propaganda literature was supplied to the organization—no more money.

In 1936, Kuhn traveled to Germany for the Munich Olympics. During his visit, he managed to secure a brief audience with Hitler. He shook hands with the führer in front of reporters and photographers. The Germans viewed the meeting merely as an official act of courtesy to the American sympathizers. Hitler made no promises and offered no support to Kuhn. Photographs of Hitler and Kuhn shaking hands appeared in American newspapers, causing quite an uproar, and gave credence to Kuhn's lies that he had the full support of Hitler for his work in America. Kuhn returned to the United States declaring that the Nazis would "wipe out the Jew pigs" someday.

The climax of the Kuhn years came in February 1939 when the Nazis held a rally at Madison Square Garden in New York City on Washington's Birthday. The meeting was threatened with attack by anti-fascist enemies of Nazis, including trade

Storm troopers and police struggling with a heckler on the platform at the Madison Square Garden rally in New York City. Fritz Kuhn stands at the rostrum during the interruption of his denunciation of Jews.

Nazism Comes to America

unionists, leftists, and Jewish war veterans. A security force of two thousand New York policemen and three thousand Nazi storm troopers protected the gathering. Nazi banners and huge pictures of George Washington and Adolf Hitler decorated the hall. Speakers compared the first American President to Adolf Hitler.

This huge show of Nazi strength only added fuel to the fires of anti-Nazi sentiment in the liberal and left press, which raised the specter of Nazi subversion at home. Again, the success of the American Nazi movement proved detrimental to the interests of the Nazi homeland.

Shortly after the rally, Kuhn was indicted for embezzling Bund funds and wound up in Sing Sing prison. From 1939 onward the Bund lost strength and influence. By the time the United States entered the war in December 1941, the Nazi movement in America had dwindled to inconsequential size.

THE FAILURE OF NAZI PENETRATION IN THE UNITED STATES

Nazi efforts to gain widespread popular support among German-Americans failed miserably. Immigrants to America have long exhibited a tendency toward strong patriotism to their adopted homeland. And the German immigrants were no exception. During World War I, there was an outbreak of anti-German hysteria directed against German-Americans in the Midwest who were suspected of harboring loyalties to the Kaiser. This

THE NEO-NAZIS

was not a pleasant period for German-Americans, but in the long run, it seemed to heighten efforts of German-Americans to separate themselves from the German state, no matter who was in power there, and to make it clear that what they cherished was their cultural heritage.

Americans in general were deeply disturbed by the vicious racism that emerged in Nazi Germany and the introduction of intolerance and censorship in a nation that had long been an important intellectual center. With the rise of the Bund, antifascist liberal and radical writers and commentators began to attack what they viewed as an appearance in America of the social insanity that had taken hold in Germany. Bundists, with their ridiculous aping of Nazi ceremony and regalia, were fiercely attacked in the press. Sensational stories portrayed them as a significant threat to American democracy. Bundists were described as "scum," illiterate "thugs," and "social misfits."

Nazism never caught on with significant numbers of U.S.-born German-Americans or those naturalized before 1900. About 90 percent of the Bund members were Germans who had immigrated to the United States after World War I. In the early thirties Hitler had high hopes for German-Americans, but by 1945 that optimism had given way to despair. Hitler came to believe that German-Americans had "become enemies more implacable than others.... Transfer a German to Kiev, and he remains a perfect German. But transfer him to Miami, and you make a degenerate out of him—in other words, an American."

Nazism Comes to America

With the defeat of Germany in 1945, the true horrors of Nazi rule became clear. Soon a new rivalry developed, between the Western bloc, led by the United States, which had emerged from the war as an economic and military giant, and the Eastern bloc, led by the Soviet Union. As attention turned to the new Cold War between these powers, many believed that the Nazi doctrines were a thing of the past, discredited, rejected, and consigned to a moral and intellectual garbage heap, never to be heard again.

3
PURIFYING THE NAZI MYTH

With America's entrance into World War II, the open advocacy of Nazism in the United States totally collapsed. America was at war with Nazi Germany. Public support for Hitlerism was no longer simply controversial or unpopular; it now smacked of treason. American media had always portrayed the American Nazis as thugs and bullies. Now the media mobilized support for the war effort, describing the war as a conflict between democracy and fascism. The American way of life—freedom, democracy, and everything good—was at stake in a war against evil.

Under the circumstances, advocacy of a new order led by Hitler and a few other discredited extremists did not stand a chance. Those sympathetic to the Nazi cause were forced to keep their views to themselves, to disavow them, or to deny they had ever held them. Some of the true believers, of course, may have acted as spies and saboteurs, doing what they could to aid Germany by disrupting the American war effort. A number of German spy rings were broken up by the FBI during the war.

In other Western nations the situation for Nazi sympathizers depended on the circumstances. In nations conquered by the German army, right-wing sympathizers were asked to collaborate with the occupation forces. Some of these people held key positions in puppet regimes established by the Nazis to rule over residents.

The end of the war, of course, made it extremely difficult for anyone to espouse Nazi ideals. The liberation of the concentration camps shocked a world that had already seen too much death and destruction. After the Allied victory, the true nature and extent of the Nazi atrocities became clear. Earlier charges of mass murder and genocide had been unproven, or the proof had been withheld from the public by government officials. But now there was incontrovertible proof that millions of people had been destroyed in gas chambers and ovens. There were mountains of rotting cadavers. There were mass graves in which the bodies of hundreds of thousands of murdered Jews, Poles, Gypsies, communists, and socialists had been dumped. And there were hundreds of thousands of emaciated survivors to bear witness.

Evidence of the Holocaust was there for all to see. Nazi documents detailing the "final solution" of the Jewish "question" were discovered. Captured Nazi officials and concentration camp survivors described the criminal procedures of mass murder. At the Nuremberg Trials, Nazi leaders were held accountable for war crimes and crimes against humanity. Hitler was dead, his philosophy and system of government discredited. It seemed that Nazism had been banished from human society forever.

Unfortunately, however, Nazism was not dead. The first attempt to revive Hitler's doctrines came as early as 1948 in a book entitled *Imperium* by Francis Parker Yockey, an American attorney who had gone to Nuremberg to participate in the war crimes trials of Nazi leaders. During the trials, Yockey became an avid admirer of Hitler and his philosophy. In *Imperium,* Yockey took six hundred pages to restate the Nazi dogma that had just been defeated and discredited in World War II. Yockey wrote that the survival of Western civilization was threatened by humanism, capitalism, and democracy. According to Yockey, these phenomena were controlled by what he called "Culture-Distorters," who in turn were under the control of "the Church-State-Nation-Race of the Jew." Blacks and other non-whites were also deemed inferior to whites and were described as "Culture-Distorters."

In 1949 Yockey wrote the Proclamation of London for the European Liberation Front, a neo-Nazi organization that was subsequently unable to gather a significant following. This proclamation called for the revival of national socialism and the expulsion of the Jews from Europe. In 1960, Yockey was arrested for passport fraud and jailed in San Francisco. Shortly afterward, he committed suicide. A prominent American right-winger, Willis Carto, visited Yockey in prison before his death. In

Purifying the Nazi Myth

the years that followed, Carto tried to carry on Yockey's efforts to purify the Nazi image. We will return later to Carto's efforts to revive Nazism.

Another early attempt to rewrite the history of Nazism was undertaken by Paul Rassinier in France. He seems to have been the first person to deny that the Nazi regime engaged in genocide. Rassinier was a communist and a socialist before the war. The Nazis imprisoned him in a concentration camp at Buchenwald. There his political views underwent a complete transformation. In 1949 he wrote a book in which he charged that concentration camp survivors had exaggerated the atrocities committed by the Nazis. Rassinier claimed that Jewish prisoners were murdered by the *kapos*—Jews who acted as supervisors of concentration camp work details—not by the Nazis themselves.

In 1964 Rassinier wrote *The Drama of the European Jews,* in which he denied that the murder of 6 million Jews by the Nazis had ever occurred. He calculated that 4,416,108 of the Jews were actually still alive and living in Europe or Israel. And those who were murdered had probably died at the hands of someone other than the Germans.

Probably only one reputable historian ever tried to revise the commonly held view of Hitler's guilt. He was A. J. Taylor, and his book, *Origins of World War II,* was published in Germany in 1961 and in the United States in 1967. Another historian, Lucy S. Dawidowicz, however, has written that Taylor's claims in behalf of Hitler are "mild and innocuous" compared to those made in the 1980s by Nazi apologists. Taylor merely wrote that Hitler did not con-

45

sciously plan World War II and that the war was "a mistake, the result on both sides of diplomatic blunders." Taylor also acknowledged that Hitler surpassed all other contemporary world leaders "in wicked deeds." But today's neo-Nazi historical revisionists claim the Nazis do not bear responsibility for causing the war, and that they never murdered 6 million Jews. They even state that there was no Holocaust, that the Holocaust is a propaganda hoax invented by Jews.

Another controversial book that appeared in 1961 was *The Origins and Originators of World War II* by David L. Hoggan. Published in Germany by a publisher with suspected links to the Nazi movement, Hoggan's book was actually a reworked version of a doctoral thesis done at Harvard in 1948. The difference between the two versions was dramatic, however. The original dissertation was reportedly described by one of Hoggan's Harvard advisers as a "solid, conscientious piece of work, critical of Polish and British policies in 1939, but not beyond what the evidence would tolerate." But the 1960 version was, as Dawidowicz charges, "an apologia for Nazi Germany in which the English were portrayed as warmongers, the Poles as the real provokers of the war, and Hitler as the angel of peace." Hoggan's book was attacked by many historians for distorting evidence and ignoring material that contradicted his personal theories. Helmut Krausnick, director of the Institute for Contemporary History in Munich, even suggested that forged material might have been used to bolster Hoggan's case. One German historian said the book was filled with "many inane and unwarranted theses, allegations and 'conclusions.'"

According to Dawidowicz, the transformation in Hoggan's writing on Nazi Germany is attributable to the influence of a man named Harry Elmer Barnes, a historian and sociologist who was extremely critical of American policymakers throughout his life. He propounded the view that "vested political and historical interests" had conspired to make it look as though Germany was to blame for the outbreak of World War I. He became an extreme isolationist who believed that high-level government conspiracies were directing the course of history. He held Franklin Roosevelt responsible for the Japanese attack on Pearl Harbor and America's entry into the war. He even began to suspect conspiracies were afoot to block publication of his books on Western civilization.

Barnes's opposition to Roosevelt brought him into contact with an assortment of rightists and Nazi supporters. Remaining true to his isolationist and non-interventionist views, he opposed American participation in the Korean War. He began working with a variety of radical libertarians who opposed government involvement in economic life and domestic affairs in the United States and who opposed intervention overseas. "It was at this time," writes Dawidowicz, "that Barnes became interested in Hoggan's dissertation and over the years guided him straight into Nazi apologetics."

Barnes had very strong views on the Nazis. In a pamphlet called "Blasting the Historical Blackout," he insisted that even if "all the charges ever made against the Nazis by anybody of reasonable sanity and responsibility were true, the Allies do not come off much better." And in another pamphlet, "Revisionism: A Key to Peace," he wrote, "Even if one were to accept the most extreme and exaggerated indictment of Hitler and the National Socialists for their activities after 1939 made by anybody fit to remain outside a mental hospital, it is almost alarmingly easy to demonstrate that the atrocities of the Allies in the same period were more numerous as to victims and were carried out for the most part by methods more brutal and painful than alleged extermination in gas ovens." By using the term "alleged extermination" Barnes seems to imply that perhaps the Nazis never engaged in mass murder. He does not offer any evidence to support his view, however.

In the early sixties Barnes met with the French Nazi apologist Rassinier, mentioned earlier in this chapter. The meeting was arranged by Mabel Narjes of Germany, who had helped to translate Hoggan's book. Barnes arranged to have Rassinier's book, *The Drama of the European Jews,* translated into English. In a rave review of Rassinier's work, Barnes wrote that the "hoax" of the Holocaust was the work of "the swindlers of the crematoria, the Israeli politicians who derive billions of marks from nonexistent, mythical, and imaginary cadavers."

Another key figure in the attempt to rewrite the history of Nazism is Willis Carto, head of the Liberty Lobby, a right-wing organization founded in 1961 and headquartered in Washington, D.C. The

Liberty Lobby is one of the best-financed organizations publishing anti-Semitic and right-wing literature in America. It boasts the sympathetic support and cooperation of a dozen members of Congress, produces a nationwide radio program, and, through a complicated network of subsidiary companies, publishes a wide range of books, pamphlets, and a weekly newspaper.

In 1961 Liberty Lobby began operation on an estimated annual budget of $35,000. By 1968 the group's income had reached an estimated $500,000, and that figure is now around $4 million per year. In 1982 Liberty Lobby's weekly newspaper, *The Spotlight,* claimed a circulation of almost a quarter-million readers, making it the most widely distributed rightist paper in the country. *The Spotlight* is not openly pro-Nazi; it attempts to project a mainstream conservative image.

As we mentioned earlier, Carto visited Francis Parker Yockey in prison shortly before his death. He arranged for distribution of Yockey's pro-Nazi *Imperium* by Noontide Press, a Liberty Lobby subsidiary controlled by Carto. In 1966, Carto gained control of the *American Mercury* magazine, which had a fine reputation as an iconoclastic publication edited by H. L. Mencken until 1933. Under Carto's control the magazine features right-wing and pro-Nazi articles, such as Barnes's review of Rassinier's book. Advertisements for Yockey's *Imperium* appear often in the *Mercury.*

While Carto's writings often invoke images of Americanism, liberty, and patriotism, his sympathies for Nazism are no secret. According to a publication of the B'Nai B'Rith Anti-Defamation League (ADL), "In a deposition under oath during proceedings connected with a Liberty Lobby lawsuit against the ADL in October 1979, Carto stated that he agreed with the tenets of the Yockey Proclamation of London," which called for the revival of national socialism and the expulsion of the Jews from Europe. In 1966, newspaper columnist Drew Pearson published the following excerpt from Carto's correspondence:

> Hitler's defeat was the defeat of Europe. And of America. How could we have been so blind? The blame, it seems, must be laid at the door of the international Jews. It was their propaganda, lies and demands which blinded the West to what Germany was doing.... If Satan himself, with all of the superhuman genius and diabolical ingenuity at his command, had tried to create a permanent disintegration and force for the destruction of the nations, he could have done no better than to invent the Jews."

In 1969 Liberty Lobby's subsidiary, Noontide Press, published an anonymous pamphlet entitled, "The Myth of the Six Million," with an introduction by Willis Carto. The pamphlet attempted to disprove the accumulated evidence regarding the Holocaust. It included eyewitness testimony by concentration camp survivors and even Nazi officers such as the S.S. commandant at Auschwitz and the S.S. member responsible for delivery of poison gas to Belzec and Treblinka.

In 1979 Carto founded the latest link in his net-

Purifying the Nazi Myth

work of organizations: the Institute for Historical Review. The IHR focuses on encouraging scholarly attempts to revise the historical interpretation of the Nazi era, and to deny the existence of the Holocaust. At the first IHR convention over the Labor Day weekend in 1979, Carto made an introductory speech denouncing Zionism and denying the existence of the Holocaust. In January 1980 the Institute of Historical Review made headlines by offering a $50,000 reward to anyone who could present "proof" that Jews were gassed to death by the Nazis. A Long Beach, California, resident, Mel Mermelstein, whose family died at Auschwitz, responded by presenting evidence, but the IHR refused to pay him the reward. The dispute wound up in court. On October 9, 1981, the judge issued a ruling with these words: "This court does take judicial notice of the fact that Jews were gassed to death at the Auschwitz concentration camp in Poland during the summer of 1944."

In 1977 a major controversy over neo-Nazi revisionism and academic freedom erupted at Northwestern University in Chicago when it was learned that Professor Arthur R. Butz had written a book entitled *The Hoax of the Twentieth Century*. The book was published in England by Historical Review Press, a neo-Nazi publishing house. The "hoax" referred to in the title was the Holocaust. According to Butz, Jews had not been "exterminated and ... there was no German attempt to exterminate them." Butz held that the Jews who had supposedly been murdered were actually still alive. *The New York Times* carried an article describing

Butz's book in January 1977. This prompted a number of angry letters to the editor disputing Butz's claim that his conclusions were based on "painstaking research." Isaac Lewin of Yeshiva University cited a Nazi document dated September 21, 1939, which referred to the "final target." He also cited a statement by the former Nazi commandant of the notorious Auschwitz concentration camp, Rudolf Hess. On April 6, 1946, Hess said that "The final solution of the Jewish problem meant the complete extermination of the Jews in Europe."

Critics pointed out that Butz was a professor of electrical engineering, not history, and that he did not have the academic credentials to claim that he had conducted "painstaking research" to overturn the conventional historical interpretation of the Nazi era. Despite his lack of credentials in history, however, his title of associate professor at a major American university lent credence to neo-Nazi attempts to rewrite the history of the Second World War.

Jewish contributors and alumni protested Butz's presence at the university, and there were calls for Butz to be dismissed. The university, however, insisted that no matter how reprehensible Butz's views were, his right to advocate them and write about them was protected by the principle of academic freedom. Others in the academic world disputed this interpretation of academic freedom. As one professor at New York University put it, "Tenure in a university faculty implies certain stipulated responsibilities, not the least of which are academic integrity and moral rectitude.... To defend a professor's right to advocate 'whatever he pleases' is academically dishonest. Should he therefore have the right to promote the seduction of children, the 'invalidity' of Newton's laws, or Charles Manson's right to depopulate California?"

Historian Lucy S. Dawidowicz criticized Northwestern for not censuring Butz's book as "an offense against historical truth." The university sponsored a series of lectures by prominent writers on the Holocaust, including Dawidowicz, to demonstrate that it did not support Butz's revisionist views and that it recognized the historical existence of the Holocaust.

A similar incident occurred in France in 1978 when Robert Faurisson, a professor of French literature at the University of Lyons, published the first of a series of articles denying that the Nazis committed genocide. Faurisson argued that the "alleged gas chambers and the alleged genocide are one and the same lie ... which is largely of Zionist origin."

The university authorities reacted by suspending Faurisson, which prompted another argument over academic freedom. During the debate that ensued, a group of leading French historians drafted a declaration asserting that the Holocaust did occur and denouncing the neo-Nazi attempt to rewrite history. The full document was published in the French newspaper *Le Monde* on February 21, 1979. A translation of the final paragraph of this declaration appears in an article by Dawidowicz. It presents an authoritative response to the campaign to erase the memory of Nazi atrocities:

THE NEO-NAZIS

> Everyone is free to interpret a phenomenon like the Hitlerite genocide according to his own philosophy. Everyone is free to compare it with other enterprises of murder committed earlier, at the same time, later. Everyone is free to offer such or such kind of explanation; everyone is free, to the limit, to imagine or to dream that these monstrous deeds did not take place. Unfortunately they did take place and no one can deny their existence without committing an outrage on the truth. It is not necessary to ask how *technically* such mass murder was possible. It was technically possible, seeing that it took place. That is the required point of departure of every historical inquiry on this subject. This truth it behooves us to remember in simple terms: there is not and there cannot be a debate about the existence of the gas chambers."

There was a Holocaust. There was mass murder. Millions of Jews, Poles, Gypsies, and political opponents of the Nazi regime were exterminated. It did happen. Now we have to understand how those responsible—such a large number of people—could have sunk to such a barbaric level, and we have to make sure it never happens again.

4
ROCKWELL AND THE AMERICAN NAZI PARTY

The name George Lincoln Rockwell is synonymous with Nazism in America. A charismatic and flamboyant leader, Rockwell founded the American Nazi Party in 1958. It was the first openly Nazi organization to spring up in the United States since before World War II. Rockwell took full advantage of media coverage of his outrageous activities and pronouncements, and pushed himself into the forefront of a worldwide neo-Nazi network. He exercised almost complete control over his followers until he was assassinated by a dissident party member in 1967. Following his death, the Nazi organization experienced divisions among its members and began to split and splinter. It never disappeared completely, however, and from time to time has shown signs of revival. No matter how bad things got for Rockwell's movement, it has always served as a pole of attraction for unstable persons and those who hate.

THE NEO-NAZIS

George Lincoln Rockwell speaking in Lafayette Park opposite the White House in Washington in 1966.

Rockwell was an improbable choice for would-be American führer. As Nazi leader, Rockwell made anti-Semitism his stock in trade, but there is indication that earlier in his life he had plenty of personal social interaction with Jews. Rockwell was the son of a vaudeville comedian named Doc Rockwell. During the 1930s Rockwell would often spend summers at his father's vacation home in Maine where such show business personalities as Benny Goodman, Walter Winchell, Fred Allen, and Groucho Marx would visit. Many of these visitors were Jews.

There was very little in the behavior or attitudes of the young Rockwell to hint at the anti-Semitism and right-wing fanaticism that would someday take over his life. An intelligent young man, Rockwell enrolled at Brown University in 1938. He dropped out of college in his sophomore year and enlisted in the military, receiving training as a fighter pilot. Eventually he commanded a U.S. Navy fighter attack squadron based in Pearl Harbor.

After the war, Rockwell seemed to have some trouble readjusting to civilian life. He worked in a variety of fields, including jobs as a sign painter and photographer. He tried to pursue his interest in art by enrolling at Pratt Institute in Brooklyn, New York. In 1948 he won an award from the National Society of Illustrators for a poster he had done for the American Cancer Society. But shortly afterward he gave up on what seemed like a promising future as a commercial artist. He was recalled to active duty as a navy pilot during the Korean War. His first exposure to right-wing politics and anti-Semitism came during this period when an acquaintance gave him some right-wing propaganda to read. At first Rockwell apparently thought very little of the anti-Semitic literature, dismissing it as racist. However, his interest was aroused and he began to read more, including *Mein Kampf.*

Hitler's book had a profound impact on Rockwell. "I was hypnotized, transfixed," Rockwell would later write of his response to Hitler's writings. "Within a year I was an all-out Nazi, worshipping the greatest mind in 1000 years: Adolf Hilter." Following his release from the military after the Korean War, Rockwell dabbled in various careers without success. He worked for a time as a traveling salesman in the South, spending a consid-

THE NEO-NAZIS

Rockwell holding a news conference at the Arlington, Virginia, headquarters of the American Nazi Party in November 1965.

erable amount of his time discussing his hatred of Jews and blacks with people he met, and securing financial contributions for racist activities.

In 1958, he grouped together a dozen followers and announced the formation of the American Nazi Party with a sensationalist, headline-grabbing publicity stunt. Rockwell led a band of his storm troopers, decked out in full Nazi regalia, in a demonstration outside the White House. The Nazis wore brown shirts with swastikas, clicked their boot heels, and shouted "Heil, Hitler" as they carried posters bearing a racist slogan: "Save Ike from the Kikes," referring to Dwight Eisenhower, then President.

Rockwell and the American Nazi Party

The Nazis set up their "national headquarters" in a dilapidated shack in suburban Arlington, Virginia, not far from the nation's capital. Headquarters included a "Shrine Room," in which Hitler memorabilia was displayed. According to a description published by the Anti-Defamation League, a photograph of Hitler was displayed against the backdrop of a huge swastika flag in the Shrine Room. Candles flickered on either side of the führer's portrait. A neon light shaped like a swastika "hung from the ceiling and from it dangled a hangman's noose. A Jewish altar cloth was used as a doormat." Nazism now became the be-all and end-all of Rockwell's life. His personal life seemed to be shattered. He had been divorced from his first wife during the Korean War. His second wife left him during the swirl of media attention that followed the formation of the party.

Mimicking his idol, Rockwell wrote a book entitled *This Time the World,* in which he expounded his simplistic, racist views and gave his blueprint for the future. In explaining his decision to found the Nazi Party, Rockwell wrote:

> All at once, I had the answer! By being an OPEN, ARROGANT, ALL-OUT NAZI, not a sneaky Nazi—with the swastika, storm-troopers and open declaration of our intention to gas the Jew-traitors (after investigations, trials and convictions)—I would ... make an end to this filthy silent treatment, for they could never ignore NAZIS with swastika armbands and talk of gas chambers.

* * *

THE NEO-NAZIS

Rockwell's plan for governing the United States was simple: "I'd reinstate the American Constitutional Republic the way it was set up by our *authoritarian* forefathers—who were in essence nothing more than National Socialists."

During the turbulent years of the civil rights movement in the 1960s, Rockwell adapted his propaganda to win support among segregationists by stressing anti-black themes. A few examples will illustrate the racism he presented. Rockwell told his readers that "our planet swarms with colored half-apes." He told a black reporter who interviewed him that he had "never met a black nigger ... that can talk and think." He said that since the interviewer was able to ask intelligent questions, he must have had some "white blood." Rockwell saw the civil rights movement as a creation of the Jews, whom he equated with communism and evil. Of the Jews, Rockwell had this to say: "The Jew has made it his life work, his burning desire to bring down, to destroy our noble Nordic race."

Like many neo-Nazis, Rockwell exhibited a contradictory attitude toward the genocide practiced by Nazi Germany in World War II. On the one hand the neo-Nazis seem to feel obliged to deny that the Holocaust ever occurred, implicitly acknowledging that the extermination of millions of people is a hideous act. But at other times they say things to indicate that they really approve of the mass murder of Jews and political opponents of Nazism in the past, and that they advocate it for the future. For example, Rockwell once told an interviewer, "I don't believe for one minute that any six million Jews were exterminated by Hitler. It never happened." The American Nazi leader insisted that "the gas chambers in these concentration camps were built *after* the war—by Jewish army officers." These statements imply disapproval of mass murder and genocide, a denial that Hitler and the Nazis could have done such a thing. However, Rockwell displayed quite a different attitude toward gas chambers in the following statement:

> ... there are going to be hundreds of thousands of Jewish traitors to execute. I don't see how you can strap that many people into electric chairs and get the job done ... it seems to me that mass gas chambers are going to be the only solution for the communist traitor problem in America.

And a similar attitude is outlined in the American Program of the World Union of National Socialists, published by Rockwell in 1965. In this document he promised to "investigate, try and execute Jews proved to have taken part in Marxist or Zionist plots of treason." The program vowed "to protect the rare honest Jew from the wrath of the people" and called for a "scientific study" of what methods would have to be used "to render Jews harmless to society."

The World Union of National Socialists was an outfit Rockwell set up to link neo-Nazi groups in Europe, North America, and Latin America under his leadership. Rockwell claimed allegiance from groups in Argentina, Australia, England, Spain, and France, but since he frequently gave grossly

THE NEO-NAZIS

exaggerated estimates of Nazi Party strength, it is difficult to judge the importance of this worldwide organization. Rockwell traveled widely across the country, speaking at college campuses usually to curious but hostile audiences. His frequent attempts to hold public rallies and demonstrations often erupted into violent incidents with opponents. First Amendment controversies arose frequently between Rockwell and local officials who tried to block his demonstrations. In all, Rockwell was jailed fifteen times on various charges.

Police in Boston protecting George Lincoln Rockwell after he announced plans to picket a showing of the movie Exodus.

Rockwell and the American Nazi Party

In spite of Rockwell's flair for making headlines, the American Nazi Party never really got off the ground. Researchers from the American Jewish Committee, which monitors the activities of extremist anti-Semitic groups, estimate that over the years no more than four or five hundred people drifted in and out of the organization, despite the party's exaggerated claims. Furthermore, many of these members were petty criminals, psychologically disturbed people, and generally unreliable individuals. Rockwell used to claim that he had five hundred storm troopers under his command and a total membership of fifteen hundred, but observers believe there were never more than one hundred or so full members in the organization at any given moment. At times Rockwell may have gotten significant financial contributions from wealthy anti-Semites, but very few people wished to be openly identified with the organization.

The Nazis soon learned that not every anti-Semite and racist in America is a Nazi, or interested in becoming one. The party had great difficulty picking up a following. As Milton Ellerin of the American Jewish Committee explains, "Americans refused to embrace an alien and enemy philosophy which so recently had claimed the lives of so many of its sons and brothers and which offered nothing by way of solution to the country's problems beyond sending blacks 'back to Africa' and Jews to the gas ovens." Things got so bad for Nazi stalwarts that sometimes Rockwell and the others who lived in the barracks at party headquarters reportedly "subsisted on canned dog food."

THE NAZIS AFTER ROCKWELL

In 1967, at the age of forty-nine, Rockwell was assassinated by John Patler, a Nazi party dissident. Rockwell's death left the movement without a clear successor. Following a brief internal wrangle, one of Rockwell's trusted aides, Matt Koehl, emerged as the new American führer. Koehl changed the name of the party to National Socialist White People's Party, a change that Rockwell had intended to make before his death. The goal was to make the organization more "American" and hence more likely to appeal to homegrown racists.

Born in Milwaukee in 1935, Koehl was the son of a Hungarian of German extraction who had immigrated to the United States. At the age of thirteen, Koehl had disrupted a classroom with an impassioned defense of Adolf Hilter. He spent some time in the Marine Corps in the early 1950s, and later became active in a number of right-wing political groups, including a neo-fascist group called the National Renaissance Party.

In 1956 Koehl worked with segregationist extremist John Kasper, who stirred up anti-black violence in Clinton, Tennessee. In 1958, Koehl was a founding member of the National States Rights Party, which was against just about every minority group—Jews, blacks, Mexican-Americans, and Asians. The NSRP was opposed to all immigration to the United States except from "Nordic Europe." In 1962 Koehl joined the Nazis and rose rapidly within the tiny party to the position of "major" in the party's "Elite Guard." He was also named national secretary of the party. In a report dated September 7, 1967, American Jewish Committee Nazi watchers evaluated the new führer in this manner:

> Koehl, better educated than the run-of-the-mill ANP officers, lacks Rockwell's flair and charismatic personality. It is doubtful that he can retain the loyalties of the small scattered group of recruits who cast their lot with Rockwell, much less build the party into a viable entity.

This prediction proved quite accurate. While his organization is still the biggest and most stable of the Nazi organizations, Koehl lacked the flamboyance to keep some of the more militant elements in line. He switched the emphasis of organizational activity away from shock tactics and street confrontations toward a strategy of strengthening the organizational structure and political program. Party literature was reworked to sound less stereotyped and more American.

Koehl wanted the party to develop a mass political base so it could make a serious bid for political power. The newfound political moderation of the Nazi party did not sit well with some old-line members. In 1970, several longtime Rockwell aides bolted the organization to found groups of their own, most of which are now defunct. Since that time the movement has been characterized by a proliferation of small feuding groups. Occasional efforts to unify the groups invariably exclude Koehl's NSWPP, and have always ended in failure.

THE NEO-NAZIS

In 1973, Koehl apparently saw an opportunity to exploit the gas shortage provoked by the Arab oil embargo following Israel's military victory over Egypt in the Yom Kippur war. Believing that many Americans would blame Jews for the long lines at gas stations and the soaring prices, the Nazis reactivated the old media-oriented street tactics employed by Rockwell. Nazis clad in full uniform, with swastika armbands and jackboots, staged demonstrations in front of the White House, theaters, and synagogues, and got themselves back into the headlines.

Party members distributed literature in shopping districts in major cities around the country and opened headquarters in four cities. Nazi splinter groups soon joined the public clamor, and controversial Nazi activists once again began appearing on talk shows. Despite the success in gaining media attention, Koehl's calculated bid to use the oil shortage to gain political support and acceptance for Nazism proved to be a complete failure. In 1974, when the Nazi media blitz began to fade, the movement had made no significant inroads in the body politic.

In November 1982, Koehl again changed the name of the party—to New Order—and announced plans to relocate party headquarters to the Midwest, complaining of declining membership, lack of local support in Arlington, and financial difficulties. New Order probably has less than one hundred full-fledged members. Each member is required to pay monthly dues of twenty-five dollars and sell a minimum of fifty copies of *White Power*, the party's monthly tabloid, which reportedly has a circulation of 2,500. Members must also participate in other organizational activities. In addition, New Order has several hundred "official supporters," each of whom pledges ten dollars per month and subscribes to the newspaper. From time to time the organization has claimed local chapters in Los Angeles, San Francisco, Milwaukee, Minneapolis, Chicago, Cleveland, Virginia, and Orange County, California, but some of these branches are very unstable and short-lived and may no longer exist. When the organization has called public demonstrations, it has never been able to bring out more than twenty members. Estimates place the organization's annual income at slightly under $100,000.

While less reliant on the shock tactics of the early years, and occasionally venturing into electoral politics to field candidates for public office, New Order/National Socialist White People's Party still persists in glorifying Nazi Germany. In the summer of 1983, the organization's publication was devoted to Hitler's S.S. troops. In an editorial entitled the "Unsung Heroes of the SS," Matt Koehl wrote that "the SS men who organized, administered and guarded the concentration camps should be accorded the honor due them."

5
SPLINTER GROUPS AND KINDRED ORGANIZATIONS

It is difficult to estimate accurately the number of neo-Nazi groups in America. Groups arise, disband, merge, or disappear—seemingly overnight. Some groups are really one-man organizations operating out of a post office box, distributing anti-Semitic and anti-black propaganda. Most groups formed after the split in the American Nazi Party in 1970 have dispersed, but the leaders of those groups continue to pop up in various groups around the country. Some of the more stable Hitlerite organizations in the United States today are described in this chapter. We will also take a look at some groups that are similar to the neo-Nazis politically, but whose members avoid dressing up in storm trooper uniforms and swastikas.

THE NATIONAL SOCIALIST PARTY OF AMERICA

The National Socialist Party of America is one of the most prominent splinter groups. The NSPA was founded by Frank Collin, a member of Rockwell's National Socialist White People's Party for five years and the NSWPP's former Midwest coordinator. Collin left the NSWPP in 1970. The circumstances surrounding his departure have been disputed in neo-Nazi circles. The NSWPP insists he was expelled after it was disclosed that he had a Jewish father. Collin's mother was a Catholic, and his father is a German Jew who survived internment at the concentration camp at Dachau; he changed his name from Cohn to Collin in 1946. Collin claims he left because of policy disagreements with Koehl.

Collin attracted national attention in the late seventies when he attempted to organize a Nazi march and rally in the Chicago suburb of Skokie, Illinois. The threat of a Nazi demonstration in a small town with a large Jewish population, including an estimated seven thousand survivors of the Holocaust, created public outcry. Municipal officials enacted a series of ordinances designed to block the demonstration. This triggered a year-long legal battle in which the Nazis were represented by the American Civil Liberties Union, which claimed that, despite their despicable political views, the Nazis were entitled to the same guarantees of free speech and assembly as other citizens. The Skokie ordinances

THE NEO-NAZIS

Anti-Nazi demonstrators shouting at Nazis rallying behind police lines in Chicago's Federal Plaza.

were eventually overturned after being declared unconstitutional. The Nazis, however, were persuaded not to hold their provocative demonstration in Skokie because of the threat of possible violence. Instead, twenty-five uniformed adolescent Nazis held rallies at Chicago's Federal Plaza on June 24, 1978, and Marquette Park on July 9, 1978, as thousands of anti-Nazis staged angry counterdemonstrations.

The full implications of the civil liberties issues raised in the Skokie case are discussed in detail in Chapter Ten. Whatever the merits of the civil liberties dispute, one thing is certain: the Skokie controversy gave the NSPA considerably more media attention than its size or influence warranted. Collin, like Rockwell, became a media personality, and was much in demand for public appearances.

On November 3, 1979, a left-wing group sponsored a demonstration in Greensboro, North Carolina, as part of a series of protests against the Ku Klux Klan's activities. A carload of Klansmen and Nazis drove to the scene of the demonstration and opened fire on the demonstrators from close range. Some of the demonstrators apparently were armed and returned fire. Five of the demonstrators were killed. Six men—four Klansmen and two members of the North Carolina branch of the NSPA—were tried for the shootings. Despite videotape recordings clearly showing the defendants firing on the demonstrators, an all-white jury acquitted them on state charges of murder and felonious rioting. A federal trial, in which the defendants were charged with violating the civil rights of the murdered demonstrators, also ended in acquittal. The failure to punish the Nazis and Klansmen involved in the shooting incident has sparked outrage around the country.

After these shootings, six Nazis plotted to commit a series of terrorist bombings in Greensboro if their comrades were convicted for the deaths of the anti-Klan demonstrators. They reportedly planned to blow up a factory, a shopping mall, and part of Greensboro's downtown district. All six were convicted on conspiracy charges in 1981.

In March 1980, NSPA chief Frank Collin pleaded guilty to charges of sexual indecencies "with a number of young boys aged eleven to fifteen" and was sentenced to seven years in prison.

Following Collin's imprisonment, leadership of the NSPA fell to Harold Covington, organizational leader in North Carolina. Covington achieved national attention in 1980 when he ran for state attorney general in the Republican primary, racking up 45 percent of the vote.

Under Covington, NSPA headquarters was transferred to Raleigh, North Carolina. The organization claims local branches in nine states and has a number of chapters in North Carolina. Like the NSWPP, the NSPA has directed considerable effort toward establishing links with Nazi groups in other countries. In 1980, representatives of neo-Nazi groups from Britain and Canada participated in the NSPA Party Congress. Covington left the organization in April 1981 under unclear circumstances and was replaced by Michael Allen, a Nazi leader from Chicago. Allen captured media attention for the NSPA in 1981 with his public acknowledgment that John W. Hinckley, Jr., the mentally ill young man who shot President Ronald Reagan on March 30, 1981, was a former member of the National Socialist Party of America. Allen told reporters that Hinckley had been expelled in 1979 because "he wanted to shoot people and blow things up."

After the Hinckley publicity, things began to go downhill for the NSPA. There were leadership changes. The organization's name was changed to the American Nazi Party, and there were splits. One faction, headed by Dennis Milam, operates under the name American Nazi Party (not to be confused with the original American Nazi Party organized by George Lincoln Rockwell) and another is known as the America First Committee, reportedly headed by Arthur Jones.

THE NSDAP-AO

The National Sozialistische Deutsche Arbeiter Partei Auslands Organization (German for National Socialist German Workers Party Overseas Organization) is primarily a neo-Nazi propaganda outfit led by Gary Rex (Gerhard) Lauck. Though he has only four or five youthful followers, Lauck is reportedly "responsible for much of the pro-Nazi propaganda currently disseminated in the United States and West Germany." Lauck has also been active in the NSPA, but lost an internal dispute with Covington in 1981 concerning leadership succession. According to Lauck, "My goal is to live to the day when no Jew holds a position of influence anywhere in the world."

Because the publication of Nazi material is illegal in West Germany, authorities believe that much of the neo-Nazi material distributed in that country can be traced to Lauck's group. Lauck himself claims links with underground neo-Nazis in Germany today. He has visited West Germany on a number of occasions. In 1972 he was arrested for violating West German laws against the distribution of Nazi literature. In 1976 he was arrested again in West Germany for transporting twenty thousand neo-Nazi posters and spent four months in jail. Afterward he was banned from that country for life. However, the ban was lifted in 1979 in order to permit him to travel to Germany to testify as a defense witness in the trial of neo-Nazis. Lauck has received considerable publicity, including an appearance on CBS-TV's *60 Minutes*. His organization is one of the tiniest, but his propaganda efforts are quite far-reaching.

NATIONAL SOCIALIST WHITE WORKERS PARTY

The National Socialist White Workers Party is based in San Francisco and led by Allen Vincent, an ex-convict and former leader of the Rockwell Nazi Party's youth group and San Francisco chapter. According to American Jewish Committee reports, Vincent has "served more than ten years in various California prisons and eleven months in the State Mental Hospital for the Criminally Insane." Vincent's group achieved some local notoriety in 1977 when it briefly operated the Rudolf Hess Bookstore—named for the German Nazi official still imprisoned at Spandau Prison for war crimes—in a Jewish neighborhood in San Francisco.

THE NATIONAL SOCIALIST LIBERATION FRONT

The most violent of the neo-Nazi splinter groups is the National Socialist Liberation Front. The NSLF was founded in 1974 by Joseph Tomassi, former West Coast leader of Rockwell's Nazi Party. Tomassi gathered a number of disgruntled ex-

NSWPP members, some with prison records, and proclaimed a commitment to "armed guerrilla struggle against the Jew Power structure." In a 1975 newspaper interview, Tomassi claimed credit for bombing a West Coast headquarters of the leftist Socialist Workers Party. In Tomassi's own words, published in the organization's publication, "We view armed struggle as the only effective means of forcing political change." According to Tomassi, the NSLF does "not wish for law and order, for law and order means the continued existence of this rotten, rip-off, Capitalist Jew System." Tomassi met a violent death at the hands of an eighteen-year-old member of the NSWPP on August 15, 1975. However, the organization continues to glorify violence even without Tomassi's leadership.

In 1983, the NSLF's newspaper, *Defiance,* carried an article praising as heroes the Nazis and Klansmen involved in the shooting of anti-Klan protestors in Greensboro, North Carolina in 1979. Tomassi's successor as head of the NSLF was David C. Rust, who was later imprisoned for violating federal firearms laws. The current leader of the organization is Karl Hand, Jr., who resigned from the leadership of the NSPA in Buffalo, New York, to assume the job of "commanding officer" of the NSLF in February 1981.

Hand explained his switch of allegiance by pointing out that the efforts of the NSPA to mobilize mass actions always ended in failure, including a rally in Buffalo on Martin Luther King's birthday organized by Hand to celebrate "white power." That rally attracted only one participant. In contrast, according to the Anti-Defamation League, Hand said that the NSLF is a "revolutionary movement that has repudiated mass tactics and had instead embraced armed struggle and political terrorism." In April 1983, Hand began serving a three-month prison sentence for a 1980 incident in which Hand and a young sympathizer of the Ku Klux Klan fired shots into the home of a black family in Barnegat, New Jersey.

In January 1984, the NSLF claimed to have acquired a copy of the Philadelphia mailing list of the militant Jewish Defense League. It published the names and addresses of the JDL members in its newspaper. The newspaper also carried an advertisement for an organization headed by Manfred Roeder, a notorious West German neo-Nazi leader, currently in prison in that country for anti-Semitic activity. Another advertisement in the newspaper was for a book entitled *Jewish Ritual Murder,* which described "the Jewish craving for spilling Aryan blood."

NATIONAL SOCIALIST LEAGUE

The National Socialist League is the only neo-Nazi group that identifies itself as a "homophile," or gay, group. Other Nazi groups refuse to have anything to do with the NSL. The group was founded in 1974 by several former members of the Rockwell group. It insists that it is not a party, but a "league" with the goal of disseminating Nazi literature within the right-wing gay community. The NSL believes that the ostracized position of homo-

Splinter Groups and Kindred Organizations

sexuals in society is the result of a Jewish Communist plot. According to the NSL:

> A key tactic of our nation's Communist and Jewish enemies is to fragment White society by turning women against men; the young against the old; the poor against the rich; consumers against producers; workers against employers; civilians against soliders; heterosexuals against homosexuals—all the while denying that race itself is a valid source of unity or a meaningful point of difference.

The NSL leader is Robert Veh who, according to the American Jewish Committee, "served time in prison for mail fraud." The group claims branches in San Diego, Los Angeles, and San Francisco, and publishes a quarterly newspaper called *National Socialist Mobilizer*. Articles in the *Mobilizer* put forth such views as "Inflation is Jewish" and "our government is almost totally Jewish." The NSL even goes so far as to imply that a Jewish conspiracy was responsible for the assassinations of prominent American political figures. The following passage from an article by NSL leader Veh gives an example of a frequently employed Nazi tactic—the matter-of-fact use of smear and innuendo without offering a shred of evidence or argumentation to substantiate allegations made:

> [If white and black leaders] don't do the Jews' bidding, they are quickly taken care of, either through scandal, such as Nixon, Agnew, Clayton Powell and others. Or they are eliminated as the

THE NEO-NAZIS

Kennedies [*sic*], Martin Luther King, Malcolm X, Medgar Evers and many others.

Without offering any proof, the Nazis imply that Jewish-led conspiracies were responsible for the murder of John F. Kennedy, who was actually killed by Lee Harvey Oswald; Martin Luther King, Jr., who was killed by James Earl Ray, a racist; Malcolm X, who was assassinated by members of a rival Black Muslim sect; Medgar Evers, who was slain by a segregationist; and Robert Kennedy, who was shot by Sirhan Sirhan, an Arab. The Nazi notion that Jews were responsible for these political murders is particularly preposterous in view of the fact that all of the victims, with the exception of Malcolm X, enjoyed widespread support in the American Jewish community. And at the time of his death, Malcolm X was in the process of developing strong political ties with leftist groups in the United States, which the Nazis have always insisted were Jewish organizations.

NATIONAL SOCIALIST MOVEMENT

One of the smallest neo-Nazi groups is the National Socialist Movement, based in Cincinnati, Ohio, led by Robert Brannen. Like other leaders of the Nazi splinter groups, Brannen is a former associate of George Lincoln Rockwell. NSM literature frequently advocates violence and chides other neo-Nazi groups for not doing enough to build a united movement to fight against Jews and blacks. The American Jewish Committee quotes Brannen as saying that "the only way to deal" with Jews and blacks "is through the barrel of a gun," and calling for "death to all Jew traitors." A leaflet distributed by the NSM featured a picture of a swastika and a gun with a message declaring that "The future belongs to the few of us still willing to get our hands dirty."

Brannen was also said to have boasted that his organization serves as "a beacon for those like [Frederick] Cowan in New Rochelle." Cowan was a member of the ultra-right-wing National States Right Party. A Nazi enthusiast, he had tattoos of the Iron Cross and the S.S. thunderbolt on his body, and he owned a collection of Nazi memorabilia, posters, books, and guns. In February 1977, when Cowan was thirty-three years old, he was suspended from his job at a moving company by a supervisor who happened to be Jewish. Cowan responded to the disciplinary action by arming himself with a hunting knife, a rifle, and four pistols. Then he drove to his company offices and went on a murderous shooting spree that left five innocent men dead, including a policeman. After being surrounded by three hundred law-enforcement officers for several hours, and ignoring pleas from his family to surrender peacefully, Cowan committed suicide. It is this kind of person that the NSM identifies with.

SECURITY SERVICES ACTION GROUP

The Security Services Action Group named after Hitler's elite S.S. troops, who guarded the concentration camps, is one of the newest American groups. Originally the Detroit branch of the National Socialist Movement organized in 1979, the group broke away from the NSM and went into the hate business on its own. The S.S. Action Group makes up for its small size (less than fifty members) by engaging in militant street confrontations with anti-Nazis in the Detroit area. Members frequently appear in Nazi uniforms. They sport Nazi-style helmets, swastika armbands, and on their collars, S.S. lightning bolts. Their demonstrations have provoked violent clashes with anti-Nazis. In 1982, S.S. Action Group members showed up at a pro-Israel rally carrying signs with deliberately offensive slogans. One sign said, "Hitler was right." In 1983, members of the group fought with two hundred counterdemonstrators at Ann Arbor City Hall in a fracas that resulted in nine arrests and injury to a policeman. It is a small but noisy group.

NATIONAL ALLIANCE

The National Alliance is among those neo-Nazi groups that rely less on Nazi regalia and more on propaganda efforts. Its origins can be traced back to the 1968 presidential campaign of Alabama Governor George Wallace. The alliance is a spin-off of the Youth for Wallace movement. Following the 1968 election, the group called itself the National Youth Alliance and stated its goal as "liquidat[ing] the enemies of the American people." It was heavily influenced by Willis Carto, founder of the Liberty Lobby, one of the best financed and organized ultra-right-wing pro-Hitler organizations in the United States, described elsewhere in this book. However, Carto soon lost his control over the youth group. In 1970 it was reorganized as the National Alliance, largely under the leadership of former activists in the Rockwell Nazi Party.

The key person in the National Alliance is William L. Pierce. A former assistant professor of physics and the holder of a Ph.D. in that subject, Pierce has long been involved in extreme right-wing politics. He was for a time a member of the John Birch Society. In 1965, he resigned from the society and from his academic post to work with George Lincoln Rockwell in the American Nazi Party. One of the few members of the party with academic credentials, Pierce was named editor of the *National Socialist World.* This quarterly journal, published by Rockwell's World Union of National Socialists, was intended to legitimize Nazism to the intellectual community. Rockwell was lavish in his praise of Pierce's efforts. When Matt Koehl became party führer in 1967 after Rockwell's assassination, Pierce was named chief ideological officer and executive assistant.

In the course of the party's internal upheavals and resultant splintering in 1970, Pierce broke with Koehl and went to work with the National Alliance which, according to *The Washington Post,* had been reorganized largely by "defectors from the old American Nazi Party." Today the group is small but extremely active in the distribution of neo-Nazi propaganda, including Hitler's *Mein Kampf,* Yockey's *Imperium,* and a variety of anti-Semitic pamphlets and material allegedly "exposing" the "hoax" of the Holocaust. "Who Rules America," a leaflet widely distributed by the group, claims that "Jewish control of the American mass media is the single most important fact of life, not just in America, but the whole world today."

In the early 1980s, the National Alliance was locked in a legal battle with the Internal Revenue Service, which sought to deny the group status as a tax-exempt non-profit educational organization. In June 1983, the U.S. Court of Appeals upheld the IRS ruling that the National Alliance was not an educational organization. The court concluded that the organization "repetitively appeals for action, including violence ... to injure persons who are members of named racial, religious, or ethnic groups."

LIBERTY BELL PUBLICATIONS

References to the Liberty Bell usually evoke images of Jeffersonian democracy. Liberty Bell Publications, however, is dedicated to publishing material that is anything *but* democratic. Located in Reedy, West Virginia, Liberty Bell is one of the leading publishers of neo-Nazi and anti-Semitic propaganda in the entire world, grinding out Nazi hate literature in English, German, French, and Spanish.

The founder of Liberty Bell Publications is George P. Dietz, who immigrated to the United States from Germany in 1957. The son of an S.S. leader, Dietz has boasted that both he and his wife were members of the Hitler Youth during the years of the Third Reich. According to the American Jewish Committee, Dietz "is contemptuous of American Nazis who ... wear 'Hollywood-style uniforms ... swagger, and look pretty tough by MGM standards.'" Dietz has always advised his followers not to wear Nazi uniforms or identify the movement's goals with Germany. According to one report, Dietz has written, "We must convince our fellow white Americans that National Socialism, which today calls itself White Power, is as American as the Stars and Stripes, motherhood and apple pie."

In line with this strategy, in the early seventies, Dietz set up a neo-Nazi outfit called the White Power Movement. He published two magazines, *White Power* and *The Liberty Bell.* Both were ultra-rightist and anti-Semitic. The main difference between the two was that *White Power* carried pro-Nazi articles, featured the swastika, offered Hitlerite literature for sale, and reported on the activities of neo-Nazi groups around the world, while *Liberty Bell* did not. Today *White Power* is defunct, however, and Liberty Bell Publications offers for sale such titles as *Mein Kampf, Hitler Was My Friend, The Hitler We Loved and Why,* and *The Myth of the Six Million,* as well as a full line of anti-Semitic bumper stickers.

ARYAN NATIONS

Aryan Nations is an organization that contributes a unique combination of religion and neo-Nazi rituals and political philosophy to the outermost fringes of the political right. This is true despite the fact that Hitlerian Nazism was fundamentally antireligious in nature. The organization is led by the Reverend Richard Butler of the Church of Jesus Christ Christian, and operates from a rural colony located on Butler's ranch in Hayden Lake, Idaho. Despite grandiose claims of 6,000 followers dispersed throughout the nation, most observers put the group's membership at around 150 persons.

Butler's theology, like that of a number of other far-right Fundamentalist Christian groups, encompasses the "Identity" doctrine. This religious dogma holds that the historical identification of Jews as the "true Israel" or the chosen people of God is false. The "true identity" of Israel is said to be the Anglo-Saxon people of Great Britain and the United States. This theology is a revival of Anglo-Israelism, a religious movement that arose in Britain in the nineteenth century. Adherents claimed that Anglo-Saxons were really the Ten Lost Tribes of Israel.

Another tenet of Butler's theology is the belief in the superiority of the white race. Non-whites are regarded as animals and are therefore said not to possess souls. Jews are even lower than non-whites; they are seen as descendants of Satan. The basic doctrines subscribed to by the Aryan Nations are shared by several other Christian rightist groups; they include the Christian Defense League, the Christian Patriots Defense League, the Covenant, the Sword and the Arm of the Lord, and Posse Comitatus. Some of these groups believe that America

Splinter Groups and Kindred Organizations

Reverend Richard Butler photographed in 1984 in his church at Hayden Lake, Idaho, headquarters of the Aryan Nations group.

is on the verge of a gigantic race war and that the second coming of Jesus Christ is approaching. In order to survive the expected race war, some of these groups have established "survivalist" camps in rural areas. They have stockpiled food, weapons, and ammunition in these camps where members can seek shelter and hold off outsiders by violence if necessary.

According to writer Peter Lake, who infiltrated the neo-Nazi movement and attended ceremonies at the Aryan Nations compound, a sign at the main gate reads "Whites Only." A double-edged sword with two swastikas on the handle adorns the altar of Butler's church. The stained-glass windows behind the altar contain the Aryan Nation's symbol, which features a modified swastika.

Pamphlets published by the group call upon followers to destroy "the lying murdering Jews," and threatens death as a penalty for miscegenation (mixing of races). According to an article in a 1982 issue of the *Aryan Nations Newsletter,* the group's ultimate goal is the establishment of a racist state by violent means:

> We will have a national racial state. We shall have it at whatever price is necessary. Just as our forefathers purchased their freedom in blood, so must we.... We will have to kill the bastards.

Aryan Nations has extensive ties with other neo-Nazi and Ku Klux Klan groups and individuals, a number of whom have participated in Aryan Nations congresses and meetings. Butler also has been

Splinter Groups and Kindred Organizations

in contact with the German activist Manfred Roeder, who reportedly has ties to Nazis in hiding in Latin America and neo-Nazi groups throughout the world. Roeder is currently serving a thirteen-year prison sentence for his role in a terrorist bombing of a Vietnamese refugee center in Germany and for Nazi propaganda activities. Traudel Roeder, wife of the imprisoned Nazi, attended Aryan Nations congresses in 1982 and 1983.

The organization received considerable media attention early in 1985 with the disclosure that as many as ten individuals linked to the Aryan Nations had been arrested in a series of violent crimes the previous year. In April 1984, an armored car had been robbed of $500,000. In June, Alan Berg, a Jewish radio performer, was gunned down in Denver. In July, $3.5 million dollars was stolen in another armored-car robbery. In November, two former Aryan Nation members shot it out with FBI agents. One died and one was captured. In searching his house, FBI officials discovered a weapons cache which included the weapon that had killed Berg. Videotapes showed members using a picture of former Israeli prime minister Menachem Begin for target practice. In December, another former member died in another shootout with the FBI. The organization denied any connection with these crimes.

NATIONAL STATES RIGHTS PARTY

Combining elements of neo-Nazism and Ku Klux Klan–style racism, the National States Rights

THE NEO-NAZIS

Party has been described as a "hybrid" organization acting "as a bridge between these two bastions of organized bigotry." The NSRP was organized in 1958 as a "white racist political party." It chose as its official emblem the thunderbolt, once the emblem of the Hitler Youth movement in Germany. However, the NSRP avoids the theatrical antics and costumes of the neo-Nazis, and employs a style of operation more in tune with the genuine, homegrown American racism pioneered by the Klan. With a membership estimated at less than a thousand and a newspaper with a circulation of fifteen thousand, the NSRP appears to have considerable influence among Klan members in the South.

One of the principal leaders of the party has been J. B. Stoner, a man with a long career in the hate movement. In the early 1940s, Stoner was an organizer for the KKK. In 1945, he organized an openly "anti-Jewish" political party composed of Klan associates, which had as its slogan: "Free America from the Jews!" Stoner told reporters in July 1946 that Adolf Hitler was too moderate in his policies. Stoner proposed "to make being a Jew a crime punishable by death." In 1959, Stoner signed on with the National States Rights Party and made opposition to the civil rights movement the focus of his political efforts.

In 1966 Stoner pleaded the Fifth Amendment during an appearance before a congressional committee investigating Klan activity. In his capacity as an attorney, Stoner has represented defendants in racial violence cases, including four Klansmen charged with a racist bombing in Florida. He also

Splinter Groups and Kindred Organizations

The Sixteenth Street Baptist Church in Birmingham, Alabama, after the bomb explosion in which four little girls were killed.

defended James Earl Ray, convicted assassin of Dr. Martin Luther King, Jr. Stoner himself was indicted in 1977 for his role in the bombing of a black church in Birmingham. He was subsequently convicted and sentenced to ten years in prison. Following an unsuccessful appeal, he jumped bail and went into hiding as a fugitive. Stoner finally began serving his sentence in January 1983.

Another prominent racist agitator affiliated with the NSRP over the years was the Reverend Connie Lynch, an official spokesman for the NSRP who frequently advocated anti-black violence during the civil rights movement. In September 1963, four little black girls were killed in the bombing of a Birmingham church during Sunday School services. This racist murder stirred the conscience of the American people. Hundreds of thousands of Americans—black and white; Protestants, Catholics, and Jews—participated in memorial services and rallies throughout the country. Political, labor, and community leaders denounced the poison of bigotry that had resulted in the murder of four children.

The reaction of the Reverend Connie Lynch of the National States Rights Party was quite different. The ADL reports that "Lynch was quoted as saying, 'If there's four less niggers tonight, then I say good for whoever planted the bomb.'"

The NSRP support of anti-black violence sometimes took the form of more direct involvement. Violent white mobs attacked civil rights demonstrators in St. Augustine in July 1964. A Florida legislative committee later identified the NSRP, Lynch, and Stoner as having significant responsibility for causing those disorders.

In 1965, Lynch reportedly told a crowd at an NSRP rally that "If it takes killing to get the Negroes out of the white man's streets and to protect our constitutional rights, I say, yes, kill them." Later that night a black man was shot and killed. Hubert Damon Strange, a white man who attended the NSRP rally, was tried and convicted of second-degree murder for the shooting. Stoner was his defense attorney.

At a rally in Baltimore in 1966, Lynch told the

Splinter Groups and Kindred Organizations

audience, "I'm not inciting you to riot—I'm inciting you to victory." The crowd then began to chant, "Kill the niggers!" Afterward gangs of white teenagers left the rally and ran through the streets attacking blacks. Lynch and several NSRP associates were convicted of inciting a riot, conspiring to riot, and disorderly conduct. They were sentenced to two years in prison.

In 1968, Stoner wrote a newsletter article calling on whites to arm themselves for a racial civil war against blacks and Jews:

> If the politicians in office were honest and not controlled by the Jews, they would be calling upon all White Christians to arm themselves and stock up on ammunition instead of trying to disarm law-abiding citizens.... Since racial civil war is already raging in America in its early stages, we Whites would be fools to ignore it. This civil war is not along geographical lines; it is not North versus South. It is a civil war with loyal White Christian Americans on one side and the Jews, Communists and blacks on the other side. The object of the Jews and Negroes is to enslave or exterminate every White person in America.

In 1972, an article published in NSRP's newspaper, *Thunderbolt*, denounced Jews as "The Enemy Within" and argued that "Every Jew who holds a position of power or authority must be removed from that position. If this does not work, then [we] must establish [the] Final Solution!!!" In Nazi parlance, of course, the "final solution" means genocide, mass murder in gas chambers and ovens.

THE NEO-NAZIS

Though its most visible national leader, Stoner, is in prison, the NSRP continues to be an important element in the ultra-right political movement. The organization has sought to develop ties with neo-Nazis in Europe and the United States. The *Thunderbolt* is widely read among Ku Klux Klanners, and plans are reportedly under way to increase membership in party branches throughout the South.

6
NEO-NAZIS AND ELECTORAL POLITICS

Despite their contempt for democracy, the neo-Nazis and other extremists and racists of the right have not hesitated to take advantage of the electoral process to spread their message in America. Running a candidate for public office offers them access to the mass media that these groups might not otherwise have.

J. B. Stoner of the ultra-right NSRP pioneered this tactic in the 1970s, campaigning for the Democratic nomination for governor and U.S. senator in Georgia on several occasions. In 1970 he won 2.2 percent of the vote, or 17,600 votes, in a bid for the governorship. In 1972 he gained 40,600 votes for 5.7 percent of the total cast in the Senate race. In 1974 he got 9 percent of the vote in the race for nomination as lieutenant governor. In 1978 he won 5 percent of the vote in the gubernatorial primary. In the 1980 race for the Senate nomination, his share dropped to 1.9 percent, following news of his conviction for a 1958 church bombing in Alabama. But more important than the vote totals was the chance to speak his racial poison to a wide audience. In his 1972 campaign he broadcast this message:

> I am J. B. Stoner. I am the only candidate for the United States Senate who is for the white people. I am the only candidate who is against integration. The main reason why the niggers want integration is because niggers want our white women.... Vote white.

Civil rights organizations protested that these racist campaign commercials were an abuse of the right to free speech, but the Federal Communications Commission refused to bar the messages and upheld Stoner's right to broadcast his views. He employed similar commercials in the 1978 campaign. The NSRP deliberately decided not to tone down its rhetoric or moderate its image in its political campaigns so that if it ever won at the ballot box it "would have a mandate" to carry out its racist program.

The neo-Nazi groups have used the electoral tactic in a slightly different manner. Their main goal tends to be gaining respectability. They usually tone down their pro-German Nazi rhetoric and often downplay party affiliation. Nazi candidates run more as anti-black racist candidates than as Hitler-worshiping Nazis.

In the first Nazi electoral foray, George Lincoln Rockwell ran for governor of Virginia in 1965 on an anti-black program, receiving some six thousand votes. For Nazi candidacies in Chicago, 1975 was a big year. The National Socialist Party of America fielded a total of three candidates, who ran unsuccessfully for alderman seats on the City Council. Frank Collin received 16 percent of the vote in Chicago's Fifteenth Ward. Thomas McGovern won 10 percent of the vote in the Eighteenth Ward and finished third in a field of six candidates. Thomas Goodwin finished with only 5 percent of the votes in the Twelfth Ward.

The NSPA's greatest accomplishment at the ballot box came in North Carolina in 1980. Harold Covington, the party's leader in that state who succeeded Collin as party commander in 1980, had run for office on several previous occasions, always going down in dismal defeat. In 1978 Covington had received only 885 votes in the Republican primary for a state legislative seat, and in 1979 he got only 172 votes out of 24,000 when he ran for mayor of Raleigh. However, in May 1980 he stunned the Republicans in North Carolina by receiving 56,000 votes, or 42.8 percent of the popular vote in a race for the Republican nomination for state attorney general. In forty-five of North Carolina's one hundred counties, Covington actually attained a majority of the votes cast. Despite having lost the election, Covington was quick to claim a moral victory for Nazism in North Carolina. He bragged that the large pro-Nazi results demonstrated that there are "many closet Nazis" in the state.

Keith Snyder, the winning nominee, said he was "appalled" that his Nazi opponent, who had run a minimal campaign and spent less than $200 on the race, had received so many votes. A Republican Party official insisted that the Nazi vote was "a freak" occurrence and that many voters did not know who Covington was or what he stood for. However, publicity surrounding the Greensboro killings and Covington's vocal defense of the arrested Klansmen and Nazis had made him and his political beliefs quite well known in the state.

Matt Koehl's National Socialist White People's Party began a series of political campaign ventures in 1975. NSWPP member Wolfgang Schrodt ran unsuccessfully for City Council in Baltimore, receiving 2.5 percent of the total vote.

In 1976 NSWPP member Arthur Jones received 5.5 percent of the vote, or 4,765 of 86,636 votes cast in a nonpartisan primary in Milwaukee. In his campaign literature, Jones had openly acknowledged his Nazi affiliation. In 1976 an NSWPP candidate had polled 6.5 percent of the vote in a race for a seat on the Board of Trustees of Breckenridge Hills, a St. Louis suburb. The same year a party candidate for the San Francisco Board of Education pulled in 8,800 votes, or 5.3 percent. In 1977 two female members of the NSWPP ran for the Milwaukee Board of Education, as "White People's" candidates. Campaign literature carried the swastika and stated that both women, Sandra Osvatic and Sandra Enders, were affiliated with the Nazi movement. Both lost, but one in seven votes in the board elections was cast for an acknowledged Nazi. Avowed Nazis have also run for mayor in Galveston and Houston, Texas.

The most startling electoral performance for the neo-Nazi, ultra-right fringe groups came in 1980 when Gerald R. Carlson, a veteran member of far right organizations, including the Ku Klux Klan, the National States Rights Party, and the Detroit Nazis, actually won the Republican nomination for Congress with 55 percent of the vote in the primary in Michigan's Fifteenth Congressional District. While Carlson's campaign was disavowed by the regular Republican party organization, he ran on the same Republican ticket as Ronald Reagan in the general elections that year. He was defeated by a Democratic incumbent who pulled in 68 percent of the vote.

The surprising successes of Covington in North Carolina and Carlson in Michigan in 1980 led the Anti-Defamation League to express "deep concern" because "so many Americans considered it acceptable to cast their votes for individuals who have openly proclaimed racist and anti-Semitic views."

7
NEO-NAZISM AROUND THE WORLD

Neo-Nazism is by no means limited to the American scene. It is an international phenomenon, assuming somewhat different forms in various countries. In many ways the American Nazis seem like a collection of nuts and unstable personalities, bullies and bad boys, driven by blind racial hatred, trying to shock people with their perverse behavior. They could almost be ignored as politically harmless and insignificant if they hadn't shown a propensity to commit acts of violence. However, the neo-Nazi and neo-fascist movements in other countries are quite different, basing their politics on a much more serious historical tradition.

In the 1930s, there were relatively strong fascist movements in almost all the countries of Europe, with the exception of Great Britain. In some of these countries, such as Germany, Italy, Spain, and Portugal, the movement attracted a mass following and attained political power. In Spain and Portugal, the movement maintained its influence until well into the 1970s. In countries occupied by German and Italian forces during World War II, members of local fascist groups were elevated to government posts in the puppet regimes set up to administer the conquered peoples.

The neo-Nazi and fascist groups active in Europe today draw upon the historical experience of those movements. Many of the groups combine within their ranks veteran activists from the old fascist movements and new militants drawn to the right-wing ideology today. This provides an organic continuity with the past—a past of power, influence, and terror—that their American brethren in the neo-Nazi movement have only dreamed about, read about, or seen in movies. In this chapter we will take a look at neo-Nazism in other countries and the international network that exists.

WEST GERMANY

It is probably no surprise that there is considerable neo-Nazi activity in West Germany, where die-hard veterans and newcomers alike attempt to revive the Thousand Year Reich and the Hitlerite dream of domination and national greatness. According to reports issued by the West German government in 1980, there were twenty-three known neo-Nazi organizations scattered around the country with an estimated membership of fourteen hundred. There are legal restrictions on political activity by these groups and the publication and circulation of Nazi propaganda. These restrictions hamper their efforts, land their militants in jail on occasion, and force them underground. These groups also have shown a marked propensity for violence and acts of terrorism. In September 1980, Hans Jochen Vogel, then minister of justice of the Federal Republic of Germany, reported that in the previous twelve-month period there had been 498 convictions of neo-Nazis and neo-fascists. An additional 101 people were under indictment and awaiting trial, while investigations of 183 others were proceeding.

In 1980 a number of European countries, including West Germany, were shaken by a wave of terrorist bombings perpetrated by neo-Nazi and fascist groups. A bomb planted by neo-Nazis exploded on September 26, 1980, during the Oktoberfest in Munich just as crowds began to disperse at the end of the day. Twelve were killed and two hundred wounded. Some victims lost their legs or arms. The man who planted the bomb, Gundolf Koehler, was killed in the explosion. He was a member of a group called the Military Sports Group Hoffmann, a neo-Nazi group led by a man named Karl-Heinz Hoffman. Formed in 1974, the organization claimed eighty members and several hundred supporters. The group had been outlawed by the West German government in January 1980. Several members, including Hoffmann, were arrested following the Munich bombing, but were subsequently released. Government officials revealed that police had confiscated grenades, explosives, and even a land mine from the homes of Hoffmann group members during the investigation.

Probably the most important neo-Nazi in West

Neo-Nazism Around the World

Germany today is Manfred Roeder, a key link in the international network of neo-Nazis. He has considerable influence within the West German movement and is in contact with German Nazi leaders who fled Europe following the defeat of Germany in 1945 and sought safety in various countries in South America. He has also cultivated relationships with anti-Semitic, right-wing, and neo-Nazi groups in the United States and Europe.

Roeder is a fifty-five-year-old disbarred lawyer with a long history in the Nazi and neo-Nazi movements. According to an article published in the newspaper of the National Socialist White People's Party, Roeder's father "was a dedicated National Socialist" during the Third Reich. Roeder himself was a member of the Hitler Youth and participated in the Battle of Berlin in 1945. Roeder is the founder and leader of two neo-Nazi organizations formed during the 1970s.

One group is the Liberation Movement of the German Reich which insists that the Third Reich "continues to exist." The other organization is the German Citizens' Initiative. Roeder has led demonstrations in West Germany demanding the release of Rudolf Hess, who was convicted at the Nuremberg Trials and is the only high-ranking Nazi to remain in prison today. Roeder has played a role in the drive to revise history in order to prove that the extermination of millions of victims by the Nazis is a hoax concocted by Zionists. Such efforts led to his arrest in 1976 for distribution of a neo-Nazi pamphlet entitled "The Auschwitz Lie," which purported to prove that the Holocaust never occurred.

THE NEO-NAZIS

A "Freedom for Rudolf Hess" rally in Bonn, Germany in 1973. Hess's son, Wolf-Ruediger Hess, is on the right.

He was given a suspended jail sentence and fined a sum equivalent to $1,200.

Roeder has been quoted as denouncing the current government of the Federal Republic of Germany as a "riff-raff state" and "a republic of Freemasons and Jews." He has made clear his hatred of democracy: "Whoever is a German cannot be a democrat and whoever is a democrat cannot be a true German." He has also endorsed terrorism: "Terror is a must, if changes are to be brought about." After another brush with the law in 1977, Roeder went underground and traveled around the

Western Hemisphere cementing ties with neo-Nazis and exiled remnants of the Third Reich.

After returning to his homeland at the end of the seventies, Roeder stepped up his activities. In 1979, a publication entitled *Teutonic Unity* began appearing. Though published under the auspices of the German Citizens' Initiative, this bulletin is basically Roeder's personal "newsletter to his followers in the U.S. and Europe," as the ADL puts it. The newsletter appears in five languages: German, English, Spanish, Italian, and French, which gives an indication of Roeder's international importance and connections.

In the June 1980 issue, Roeder undertook to open a controversial discussion of a possible alliance between the Nazis and Soviet Russia, against the Western democracies. He pointed with approval to Soviet policies of anti-Zionism and anti-Semitism and questioned whether the long-standing Nazi equation of communism with Judaism was still applicable. Roeder told his readers that he was tired of hearing about the "kosher Kremlin theory" and asked instead that they address the issue of "what should real patriots do . . . If Russia was no longer dominated by Zionist Jews?" In Roeder's view, "If Russia is not in Jewish chains anymore, I would not hesitate to cooperate with them to destroy the totally Jew-dominated power of the United States, thus liberating the nearly totally enslaved people of America."

Roeder is currently serving a thirteen-year prison sentence for his role in a wave of terrorism that hit Germany in February 1980. The arson and bombing attacks launched by a group called German Action Groups were directed at memorials dedicated to war victims of the Nazis and at the shelters for refugees from Ethiopia and Vietnam. Two Ethiopians were injured in an attack on a home in the city of Loerrach, and two Vietnamese refugees died in a nighttime fire-bombing of a refugee center in Hamburg. The neo-Nazi leader continues to communicate with his supporters from his prison cell by means of newsletters and articles. His bulletins include appeals for financial support for his wife and six children. Roeder's wife, Traudel, has represented him at international neo-Nazi gatherings during his incarceration.

ITALY

A number of neo-Nazi and neo-fascist groups have operated in Italy over the past decade and a half, frequently posing a terrorist threat. While leftist terrorism in Italy by such groups as the Red Brigades has gotten much media attention, attacks by rightist elements in that country have also been numerous and costly in terms of casualties. In 1980, newspaper reports revealed that neo-Nazi and neo-fascist terrorists had claimed the lives of 132 people over the previous eleven years, and that 260 rightists were being held in prison.

In 1969, a terrorist bomb planted at a Milan bank killed sixteen people. A leading neo-Nazi, Franco Freda, received a life sentence for his role in the bombing. Freda advocated a doctrine called Nazi-Maoism, which called for unity between the ultra-

Neo-Nazism Around the World

left and ultra-right to destroy the common enemy—democracy. Freda's doctrine still has influence in the Italian right. A *Newsweek* article, published following the 1980 neo-Nazi terror wave, reported that "Professor Paolo Signorelli, a radical rightist, has publicly called for the 'union of revolutionary forces from the left and right in a single popular movement.' " And *The Economist* reported in October of 1980 that a new group called Quex "believes in the curious amalgam of Nazi and Maoist views preached by Mr. Franco Freda" and that another group called Third Position "favors a joint struggle with the far left against Italy's democracy." The Anti-Defamation League suggests that over the years ultra-left and ultra-right terror groups have been able to develop unity around their shared support of the Palestine Liberation Organization and their opposition to Israel.

Right-wing terror continued to arouse public alarm during the 1970s. In 1974, a bomb exploded at a political demonstration, taking the lives of nine persons. In August of that year an express train blew up inside a tunnel between Florence and Bologna. Twelve were killed and forty-eight wounded in this tragedy. In 1980, eight neo-fascists were arrested for the tunnel bombing. Right-wing terrorists were also blamed for a massive bomb that exploded in a train terminal in Bologna in August 1980, when it was crowded with vacationing tourists. The explosion took the lives of seventy-six people and injured two hundred others. The worst terrorist incident in Europe since the Second War World, the Bologna bombing triggered mass demonstrations in major Italian cities demanding a government crackdown on terrorists.

The main neo-Nazi and neo-fascist groups known to be operating in Italy include the Armed Revolutionary Nuclei, Revolutionary Action, the Popular Revolutionary Movement, and New Order.

FRANCE

A number of violent acts have been attributed to neo-Nazis in France since the late 1970s. These include the bombings of the headquarters of the Federation of French Jewish Societies, a youth organization in Paris, and a synagogue in a Parisian suburb as well as an arson attack on a monument to Jews murdered in the Holocaust. A neo-Nazi group calling itself the French National Liberation Front claimed responsibility for some of these incidents, which they boasted were acts "of resistance against the Jewish occupation of this country."

France, too, fell victim to the wave of neo-Nazi terror in 1980. On the same weekend as the Munich Oktoberfest bombing, machine-gun fire was directed at a number of Jewish targets in Paris, including a war victims monument, synagogues, schools, and day care centers. Shortly thereafter on October 3, 1980, a bomb exploded outside another crowded Paris synagogue, wounding twelve worshipers and killing four. Only the fact that religious services had run longer than usual averted a far greater tragedy. Normally, hundreds of people would have been outside the temple at the time the

The wreckage outside a synagogue in Paris where a bomb exploded and killed four persons in October 1980.

blast occurred. Anonymous telephone calls to French newspapers claimed that the terrorist actions had been carried out by Nationalist European Front, a neo-Nazi organization in France headed by a man named Mark Frederiksen. The Nationalist European Front was the successor to a group called the National Federation of European Action, which had been outlawed by government order on September 3, 1980. The organization reportedly

THE NEO-NAZIS

had as many as 150 members in Paris and 180 in Nice, though it is difficult to judge the accuracy of such figures.

SPAIN

Fascism triumphed in Spain in the Spanish Civil War in which Falangist forces led by Generalissimo Francisco Franco defeated the liberal-left coalition that had ruled the short-lived Spanish Republic. Many people view the Spanish Civil War as a dress rehearsal for the Second World War. Hitler and Mussolini poured money, supplies, and advisers into the country to aid the Franco forces, while communists and socialists throughout Europe sent aid, including volunteer brigades, to fight the fascists. Later, Franco avoided direct involvement in World War II and subsequently made his peace with the Western alliance. The 1970s were a decade of transition from the fascist rule of Franco to the current Spanish democracy. Ironically, a socialist today holds the position of premier, forty-five years after the overthrow of democracy by Franco. Vestiges of the past remain, however, as evidenced by an active and visible neo-fascist, pro-Nazi movement.

Spain's biggest neo-fascist political organization is Fuerza Nueva, headed by Blas Pinar. Perhaps as many as twenty right-wing paramilitary organizations have sprung up. The most important is Fuerza Joven, which may have three thousand adherents, many coming from police and military families, the last bastions of the Francoist movement. Demonstrating their neo-Nazi tendencies, these young rightists mark Hitler's birthday by gathering near military headquarters in Madrid each year. Although it is illegal, they wear uniforms bearing the swastika. The paramilitary groups reportedly receive military training from former Franco loyalists, including "at least one former Hitler S.S. officer," according to the ADL. A number of violent incidents have been attributed to rightists in recent years, including attacks on synagogues, and the killing or beating of twenty-one victims in 1980 alone.

Another important neo-fascist organization is the Spanish Circle of Friends of Europe, known as Cedade. This group was set up with the support of the Franco regime in 1960. It has more than two thousand members and maintains relations with foreign right-wing organizations. Advertisements for Cedade have appeared in American neo-Nazi publications.

BELGIUM

Belgium has the dubious honor of hosting one of the most public of the neo-Nazi and neo-fascist organizations in Europe. The Vlaamse Militanten Orde (VMO) is a Flemish group based in Antwerp and led by Bert Erickson. It claims three hundred members, a relatively large number considering the small size of Belgium. Each year the VMO sponsors a gathering at Dixmuide to honor Belgians who died during World War II in the service of the Nazi cause. The festival is attended by neo-Nazis and neo-fascists from perhaps a dozen nations. It thus serves as a key element of the international network of far right organizations. Some participants are veterans of the old days, who use the occasion to reminisce about the heyday of the world fascist movement.

The VMO actively maintains ties with like-minded organizations throughout the world. In 1980, for example, four VMO leaders traveled to Georgia to meet with members of the National States Right Party. Their visit was cut short when the U.S. government issued a deportation order. An article in the German magazine *Der Spiegel* reported that Belgian members of VMO, French neo-Nazis, and German members of the Hoffman group have participated in joint paramilitary exercises near the village of La Roche near the German-Belgian border.

Author Claire Sterling spent three years researching terrorist organizations and then published her findings in *The Terror Network* in 1981. She reported that in 1972, another Belgian neo-Nazi leader, Jean Roberts Debbaudt, offered to put his organization, the neo-Nazi Rexist Party, "totally and unconditionally" at the service of the Palestine Liberation Movement in its efforts to fight Israel. Since that time, Debbaudt has gone on to lead the Mouvement Social Belge. Sterling reports that Debbaudt served as an officer in Hitler's Waffen S.S. during the Second World War.

SWEDEN

The main neo-Nazi organization in Scandinavia is the Nordiske Rikspartiet, led by Goran Assar Oredsson and his wife Vera, who grew up in Nazi Germany. The Swedish organization was established in 1956 and has branches in several cities. In the mid-seventies, several members were imprisoned for bombing a theater.

GREAT BRITAIN

Britain has a number of neo-Nazi and neo-fascist organizations. The most successful of these groups tend to hide their Nazi pretensions and origins from public view. Instead they opportunistically exploit the racial tensions that exist between the native white population and the non-white immigrants and their descendants.

The League of St. George is openly Hitlerite, however, concentrating its efforts on keeping alive the memory of Nazism and maintaining links with other Nazi organizations around the world. The group does not believe in electoral politics, and there are rumors that the League has ties with secret paramilitary organizations that are preparing for the day when "events of catastrophic proportions will rapidly overtake civilization."

The most important of the neo-Nazi and neo-fascist groups is the British National Front. This group was formed in 1967 by the merger of several fascist organizations, including several that were openly and blatantly neo-Nazi and paramilitary. One of those founding organizations was the British National Party, which had ties to Nazism in the past. By the sixties, according to author Michael Billig, the Front was undergoing a change of orientation "from paramilitary Nazi unit to constitutional respectable quasi-party." Another founding group in the National Front was the Greater Britain Movement. Led by John Tyndall, this was "an explicitly Nazi group." According to Billig, Tyndall's group emphasized the military aspects of Nazism in its propaganda and organizational structure to such an extent "that it was a miniature copy, or parody, of a classic Nazi militia unit." Tyndall's fascination with Nazi militarism was of long standing. In 1962, Tyndall was arrested for his part in the activities of Spearhead, a paramilitary organization linked to the British National Party, of which Tyndall was a member at the time. This group, modeled after the Nazi storm troopers, held military training exercises in the British countryside. Spearhead's newspaper, *Greyshirt,* described the organization as a "fanatical core of hardened men, trained and disciplined in the struggle." Their slogan, "Victory Hail—*Sieg Heil,*"was borrowed from their Nazi forebears.

By the 1970s Tyndall had become the chairman of the British National Front. The organization has attracted considerable media attention and some measure of popular support. By 1977 the Front had become the fourth largest political party in Great Britain, threatening to overshadow the declining Liberal Party in some areas. In 1977 elections, its

Neo-Nazism Around the World

candidates polled 200,000 votes nationally, receiving 100,000 in the London area alone. In order to gain support, however, the organization has obscured its Nazi origins and beliefs. Members are forbidden to maintain active membership in the openly Nazi League of St. George, though members of the Front frequently publish articles in the League's journal. The Front avoids the use of Nazi symbols and blatant anti-Semitism in its literature. Magazines published by sympathizers and members of the Front include *The Spearhead*, published personally by Tyndall. These publications offer readers a chance to join book clubs that offer Nazi classics and anti-Semitic propaganda. The primary source of the Front's electoral success has been its skillful manipulation of racial tensions.

8
INTERNATIONAL LINKS AND PROPAGANDA

THE INTERNATIONAL LINKS

Neo-Nazis are politically isolated, existing on the far fringes of contemporary political life in most countries. But they are not isolated from one another. Nazis actively seek one another out across national boundaries. They exchange information, coordinate the distribution of propaganda, and perhaps even coordinate terrorism. In this chapter we will examine the various forms these international connections have taken.

Citing research by Claire Sterling, the Anti-Defamation League believes that efforts to build a Black International, to coordinate the activities of far right groups, began as long ago as the late fifties and early sixties. Calling itself the European New Order, after Hitler's promise of a new order for the world, "The group sought to pull together the Nazi

International Links and Propaganda

and fascist remnants of the Third Reich and Mussolini's regime, and similar leftovers from prewar and wartime Nazi and fascist movements."

Sterling says that this Black International decided to cooperate with radical left groups in attacking Israel and supporting the PLO. The members spoke of the fight against what they called "imperialzionism," which incorporated opposition to the imperialism of the capitalist democracies and to the Zionism and continued existence of the state of Israel. Mrs. Sterling reports that the European New Order agreed at a meeting in Barcelona in April 1969 to supply ex-Nazi military officers to train Arab terrorists, and to undertake a pro-Palestinian, anti-Israeli propaganda campaign in European nations. Sterling writes that three "Black Summit" meetings were held in the early seventies to promote support for the PLO. At the March 28, 1970, meeting in Paris, Jean Roberts Debbaudt offered to put his Belgian neo-Nazis at the disposal of the Palestinian movement. At the September 16, 1972, conclave in Munich, six hundred delegates came together at the First National European Congress of Youth. They applauded the Palestinian terrorists who had murdered eleven Israeli athletes at the Munich Olympics ten days earlier in the same city. The March 9, 1974, Black Summit was held in Rome, and was attended, according to Sterling, by the prime minister of Libya, representing Muammar el-Qaddafi, the Libyan dictator and patron of terrorism.

Sterling also writes that a Swiss banker, Francois Arnoud, played a key role in financing the early terrorist efforts of the PLO in Europe. A founder of Switzerland's neo-Nazi party, Arnoud has a long-standing interest in Nazi affairs. He holds rights to a book on Martin Bormann, a top Nazi during World War II, and on the posthumously published works of Joseph Goebbels, Nazi propaganda minister. According to Sterling, "As head of the Arab Commercial Bank in Geneva, Arnoud soon became a formidable financial power," and "tens of millions of dollars passed through the hands of this neo-Nazi financier for the Palestinians' use in Europe."

There are indications of neo-Nazi coordination of terrorism in Europe. As described in Chapter Seven, a wave of neo-Nazi terrorism broke out in 1980. An article in the Los Angeles *Herald-Examiner,* October 8, 1980, cited unnamed but "knowledgeable counterterror sources," which said that "the signal for neo-Nazi violence ... came early last month at coordinating conferences between the so-called Defense Sports Group of West Germany and the Revolutionary Nationalist Movement in France." The article said that two conferences had been held near Dusseldorf and one near Munich, and that PLO observers were in attendance. It went on to say that the neo-Nazi terror activities were "assisted and supported by Libya and PLO camps in Lebanon and Iraq where neo-Nazi recruits are trained alongside other international terrorists."

Other international links between European neo-Nazis include the annual festivities at Dixmuide sponsored by the Vlaamse Militanten Orde

International Links and Propaganda

and the joint military training of Belgian, German, and French groups discussed in Chapter Seven. *Der Spiegel* magazine also reports that "some 200 neo-Nazis in West German prisons regularly receive contributions from the U.S., Belgium and from a foundation administered by the former South Tirolean terrorist, Norbert Burger."

A key figure in the international neo-Nazi network was Manfred Roeder, the West German neo-Nazi currently serving a thirteen-year sentence for terrorist activities. Before his imprisonment, Roeder was a very busy man. In 1976, he visited the United States for five weeks. While he was in this country, he attended a World Congress of National Socialists organized by the New Christian Crusade Church, and he visited a number of cities, making contact with American neo-Nazis. In November 1977, Roeder fled Germany because of legal trouble and went underground. He showed up in April 1978 in Brazil at an international Nazi reunion that brought together groups from four countries in honor of Hitler's birthday. The participants were members of the Kamaradenwerk, a network of Nazis who escaped to Latin America after the fall of the Third Reich. According to the ADL, the leader of the Kamaradenwerk was Josef Mengele, a notorious Nazi war criminal. Mengele, a physician at Auschwitz concentration camp, has been accused of performing cruel and inhuman medical experiments on prisoners. Many authorities now believe that Mengele died in a boating accident in Brazil. A body found in June 1985 was identified as his.

Brazilian police raided the hotel where the meeting was held and found twenty Germans who had immigrated to Latin America after the war. They also found German-language Nazi literature in abundance, including *The Protocols of the Elders of Zion* and *Mein Kampf*. The literature was published in the United States by Liberty Bell Publications in Reedy, West Virginia, controlled by George Dietz, whose activities were described in Chapter Five. The police raid in Brazil prompted fugitive war criminal Gustav Franz Wagner to turn himself in to Brazilian authorities. Wagner was a Nazi official at Treblinka and Sobibor concentration camps, where he allegedly directed the murder of over one million prisoners and came to be known as "the human beast." Wagner apparently feared that publicity surrounding the Kamaradenwerk raid would soon lead Israeli Nazi-hunters to his hiding place. He chose to take his chances with Brazilian authorities rather than risk being spirited off to Israel to stand trial as a mass murderer.

Following the Brazilian incident, Roeder appeared in Chile, where he sent a letter to the Chilean president protesting the Wagner arrest. An English translation of his letter appeared in the *Voice of German Americans,* published in Buffalo, New York, by a group known as the Friends of Germany. The president of the Buffalo organization is Alexi Erlanger, who also circulates Roeder's *Teutonic Unity* newsletter in America. The tight web of interconnections between Roeder and certain American-based neo-Nazis can be noted by the fact that funds solicited to support Roeder's family during his imprisonment in West Germany are collected by two Americans: Dietz in West Virginia and Erlanger in Buffalo.

After his stint in South America, Roeder came to the United States. He visited Willis Carto's Liberty Lobby and William Pierce's National Alliance in Washington, D.C. Both organizations were so honored by Roeder's visit that they published articles about it in their newspapers. Roeder also made contact with Richard Butler, leader of the Aryan Nations in Idaho, and attended that organization's congress in the summer of 1980. Before leaving the United States, Roeder met with various Ku Klux Klan factions and lectured at a number of Klan meetings.

Following his imprisonment in 1981, Roeder's wife, Traudel, represented him at the 1982 and 1983 International Congresses of Aryan Nations held at Hayden Lake, Idaho. At the 1982 congress, Alexi Erlanger, the Buffalo neo-Nazi, presented Mrs. Roeder with a medal for "her courage and loyalty to her family and the German liberation movement."

In the United States, the National States Rights Party, the group that fuses the beliefs of neo-Nazis and Ku Klux Klansmen, has paid particular attention to developing international links. NSRP leaders J. B. Stoner and Edward Fields have attended several of the Vlaamse Militanten Orde's annual meetings at Dixmuide. Both men also visited neo-Nazi groups in Great Britain in 1975, 1976, and 1977. Stoner addressed a meeting of the League of St. George in 1976 and met with officials of the British movement. He also spoke at a London meeting of the National Front. In 1977, Fields was a principal speaker at Dixmuide and made time to speak at four meetings of the National Front in different cities in Britain. The NSRP hosted the October 1980 visit of Belgian neo-Nazi leaders from the VMO. Their stay was cut short when Secretary of State Edmund S. Muskie ordered the four men out of the country after their true identities were revealed. During 1979, John Tyndall, veteran British neo-Nazi and leader in the National Front, visited the NSRP. He also met with William Pierce's National Alliance and Willis Carto's Liberty Lobby, where he taped a radio interview.

The international efforts of the New Order—or the National Socialist White People's Party or American Nazi Party, as it has been known throughout its twenty-six-year history—were described in an earlier chapter.

INTERNATIONAL PROPAGANDA

The anti-Semitic propaganda distributed throughout the world by neo-Nazi and far right groups is remarkably similar. Indeed, much of literature emanates from a handful of locations. Three outfits—Gerard Lauck's NSDAP-AO, in Nebraska; George Dietz's Liberty Bell Publications in Reedy, West Virginia; and the Liberty Lobby's Noontide Press—grind out a good portion of the world's neo-Nazi anti-Semitic propaganda.

One item is distributed by virtually every anti-Semitic organization in the world and serves as the basis for modern anti-Semitic propaganda. It is

International Links and Propaganda

called *The Protocols of the Learned Elders of Zion.* This document supposedly blueprints the evil plans of world Jewry to rule the world. However, the *Protocols* was exposed as a fraud in 1921. It was *not* written by Jews. It was written by the Czarist secret police in Russia at the beginning of this century, and was designed to fuel the passions of anti-Semitism by supposedly revealing that Jews are conspiring to dominate the world. There are five basic elements in this propaganda package:

- The concept of the "chosen people" was devised to justify world domination by the Jews.
- Jews infiltrate the Freemasons in order to decieve non-Jews and carry out their conspiracy to take over the entire world.
- Jews have successfully maneuvered to take control of the global banking system and economically exploit non-Jews.
- Jews control the world's mass media and manipulate the masses for their own nefarious purposes.
- Jews plan to achieve their goal of world domination through conspiracy and duplicity.

The Protocols and the lies and myths derived from them have circulated for decades. As mentioned in Chapter Two, the American industrialist Henry Ford once arranged for a republication of the Protocols in Dearborn, Michigan. Ideas contained in the Protocols have been incorporated in the Soviet anti-Zionist propaganda campaign. Copies of the Protocols circulate throughout the Arab World. Qaddafi reportedly keeps a supply of them on his desk and gives them to visitors. A spokesman for the Palestine Liberation Organization has hailed the Protocols as "the pure truth." The material has been sold retail in the United States, Italy, Great Britain, Mexico, Panama, and Chile. It has been reprinted and circulated by neo-Nazi, neo-fascist, and anti-Semitic groups and by individuals in countries the world over, including some countries where there are no Jews. People read them and believe them despite the fact that they have been known to be a hoax for sixty years.

9
THE NAZI PERSONALITY

What kind of person becomes a Nazi?

Neo-Nazis are obviously very different from most other people. The prevailing social philosophy and moral code in a democratic society like ours places great emphasis on values like brotherhood, mutual respect, the sanctity of life, tolerance for others, social equality, and freedom. Such views are generally supported by the precepts of most religious doctrines, and indeed these values are a necessity for our peaceful existence as social beings living together in a complex network of interrelationships with different kinds of people.

We know, however, that the world is not a perfect place. Many people fail to live up to the idealistic goals of this moral credo. Prejudice, intolerance, and injustice are widespread, manifested on both the social and the individual level. Most people wrestle with conflicting feelings and values, and try to control their behavior in a socially acceptable way. No one would deny that many people are pre-

THE NEO-NAZIS

judiced; they discriminate against members of certain racial, religious, and ethnic groups. Some non-Jews are anti-Semitic; some whites hate blacks; and some blacks hate whites. This failure to live up to the values of brotherhood is disturbing, but it is important to remember that not every anti-Semite and every anti-black person is a Nazi. There is a difference between disliking, or even hating, someone because of his or her ethnic background—a prejudice that contradicts the values of society—and embracing a political and social ideology that calls for the elimination and murder of a group of people because of their ethnic background. Clearly, neo-Nazis are different. Their behavior is perverse; their values stress hatred and mistrust, power and force, racism and oppression. What makes them believe and behave this way?

The psychology of Nazism has long intrigued researchers from a variety of disciplines: history, psychology, and social psychology. Many theories of the psychology of fascism and prejudice have emerged. To the lay person the differences between these theories and their sometimes contradictory elements are not readily apparent. A full evaluation of these psychological theories is beyond the scope of this book. What we want to do here is get an idea of some of the major explanations of the fascist phenomenon and take a look at some of the empirical evidence, which might give us a picture of the kind of person who turns to Nazism.

Attention has focused on two aspects of the Nazi phenomenon: the psychology of the leaders and the psychology of those who follow them. Many observers noted that Hitler skillfully manipulated masses of people and concluded that he was a master of the psychology of group behavior. In *Mein Kampf* Hitler wrote about a number of concepts that seemed to be derived from *The Crowd* (1895; reprint 1969), an important early work on crowd behavior by social scientist Gustave Le Bon. As Michael Billig, a writer who researched neo-fascists in Britain, pointed out, Le Bon theorized about the "mental unity of crowds," which allowed a skillful leader to override rational and civilized norms of behavior. Le Bon held that crowds were highly suggestible. He also believed in the concept of "racial unconsciousness," which he said was the unifying element in the group mind, and which could be tapped and manipulated by a skillful speaker. These were pivotal points in Hitler's writings on leadership and propaganda.

Sigmund Freud, the father of psychiatry, believed that Le Bon's description of crowd behavior was accurate. In Freud's view the power of the leader lay in the fact that he represented a father figure to his followers. Social psychologist T. W. Adorno believed that Hitler and his associates had mastered the skill of manipulating the subconscious mind. Psychiatrist Wilhelm Reich believed that fascism was an expression of repressed sexuality. Some writers who have examined *Mein Kampf* believe that Hitler's political ideas stemmed from his unhappy childhood and poor relationship with his father. His early feelings became displaced and were transposed into a fanatical hatred of Jews and a boundless thirst for absolute power. Psychiatrist

THE NEO-NAZIS

Erich Fromm believed that the rise of capitalism and the destruction of the centuries-old structure of feudalism produced social instability. Certain individuals found the change difficult to deal with, especially in economically or politically unstable times. In this view fascism's mass appeal stems from its ability to provide a sense of social security. The follower finds comfort in trading the insecurity of individual freedom for the power of the leader.

It is, of course, impossible to prove any of these theories about the psychology of fascist leaders. However, it is important to try to understand the

Hitler addressing a rally of Nazi youth in Nuremberg in 1937.

psychology of the followers, those who submit to the dictates of fascist and Nazi leaders, and thereby transform their views into a social movement.

The relationship between individual psychology and fascist or Nazi membership seems to be related to how much success fascism is enjoying at any particular moment. Billig argues that when fascism is thriving as a social movement, attracting considerable support, and seriously vying for political power, individual psychological characteristics decrease in importance. On the other hand, when fascism or Nazism is a tiny minority movement, totally at odds with the rest of society, psychological characteristics seem to play a greater role in explaining why someone becomes a member. Historically, certain social conditions favor fascism: (1) a breakdown in normal institutional functioning of certain sections of society; (2) generalized political unrest; and (3) social and economic chaos. German society, especially the middle class, was in this state in the decade following the First World War. When the fascist movement is thriving, people flock to it for a variety of reasons. Many of them may not really be totally committed to the ideology: they may not be true believers. This is certainly what happened in Germany. As the Nazi movement grew in power and significance, there was a bandwagon effect. People joined something that was growing. As Nazism became more influential, some people joined to avoid social ostracism. Others were motivated by opportunism, realizing that future career opportunities in the state bureaucracies would be enhanced by Nazi membership.

THE NEO-NAZIS

The situation is completely different at a time when to be a Nazi is to be an outcast, a member of an extreme minority, totally discredited in the eyes of society at large. At such times only true believers stay in the movement. Membership is no longer the result of a bandwagon effect. To be a member is to risk ostracism, not avoid it. Membership is more likely to harm career and job opportunities than help them. Individual psychological factors driving someone toward a Nazi organization in such a period become extremely important

Following World War II, Adorno led a team of psychologists in a study commissioned by an American Jewish agency to identify the psychological characteristics of persons who were attracted to fascism. The results of this study were published in *The Authoritarian Personality,* a classic in the field. A number of the assumptions and conclusions of this study have since been questioned, but the fundamental profile of an authoritarian personality—a personality type predisposed toward becoming a follower of an authoritarian movement—persists.

The person with an authoritarian personality is seen as psychologically weak, uncertain, and insecure. He compensates for this weakness in himself, which he despises, by an extreme admiration for and identification with the polar opposites of these traits: strength and power. The authoritarian personality has both sadistic and masochistic characteristics. The masochist or self-hurting element is seen as authoritarian submission—surrendering individual freedom to the dictates of the leader. The sadistic element is called authoritarian aggression—lashing out at a scapegoat. The authoritarian personality tends to think in simplistic patterns, seeing things in black and white, ignoring shades of gray. Complexity and nuance is confusing and disconcerting. As a consequence the authoritarian personality tends to be ethnocentric, trusting only his own grouping, and mistrusting outsiders. People with an authoritarian personality structure are not necessarily fascists, but many psychologists believe that people with this type of personality are predisposed toward fascism and Nazism, particularly in a period, such as today, when such movements make up extreme minorities.

A recent study of the case histories of anti-Semitic patients by a group of psychiatrists confirms the crucial influence of early childhood experiences on the development of prejudicial attitudes. The seeds of prejudice may actually be sown in infancy, as early as seven months of age. According to child psychoanalyst Dr. Peter Neubauer, "Normal development demands that the infant bond with those who love him most by distinguishing and turning away from strangers. This stage prepares the soil for attitudes toward strangers that will come later in life." Dr. David Hamilton, a social psychologist at the University of California at Santa Barbara, explained that "Prejudice arises from a person's cognitive orientation, from the attitudes he learns and from the way these attitudes fit his psychological needs." Anti-Semitic patients included in the study had a tendency to project their own faults onto scapegoats. Patients tended to deal with their own greed, for example, by denying that they had this fault and insisting instead that they hated Jews because *they* were greedy. One male patient transformed his rivalry with his father into anti-Semitism. All the resentment he felt toward his father was expressed as complaints against Jews. He said Jews were aggressive busybodies who were always trying to control things. This man had *not* been victimized by Jews. His real problem was his inability to directly express his anger at his father.

There are no reliable studies on the psychological characteristics of neo-Nazis, partly because extremist members of neo-Nazi organizations rarely seek psychiatric help in dealing with their racism and other prejudices. We can, however, refer to the results of these studies in developing a profile of the neo-Nazi. We can also draw on journalistic reports on the activities of the neo-Nazis, and on studies of the personal background of neo-Nazis who have been arrested for committing crimes.

Recently, freelance writer Peter Lake infiltrated neo-Nazi groups on the West Coast and participated in activities at the Idaho compound of the Aryan Nations. Lake summed up his impressions of the neo-Nazis he met:

> They smoke a lot, they're paranoid beyond belief, they're friendly, they're poor, and they hate Jews more than all other racial and ethnic groups combined.
>
> Paranoia reigns as the ultimate and overriding emotion, able at any instant to transform any discussion, any conversation, any attempt at communication into a frustrating exercise in un-

founded fear. "The enemy is everywhere," I would hear again and again.

Lake also found that the neo-Nazis were fascinated by Nazi memorabilia and guns. Many photographs taken by Lake show Nazis sporting Nazi military uniforms and proudly displaying handguns and rifles.

Other insights into the type of person attracted to neo-Nazism can be drawn from a study done twenty-five years ago. Researchers interviewed 41 of 154 young offenders arrested in a wave of anti-Semitic, neo-Nazi vandalism in 1960. The subjects ranged in age from eleven to twenty-five. Only five of them had done well in school. The rest were underachievers who, though they had average or better intelligence, had done poorly in school. Fifty-four percent had police records. Ten were considered troublemakers at school. Fourteen were members of Nazi gangs. Twenty-one were members of neighborhood gangs. Twenty subjects had collections of Nazi memorabilia, and nine owned Nazi uniforms.

Interviewers asked the youths about their major interests. Uniforms, guns, and the military were common replies. Thirty-three of the youths came from broken homes and from families who had been hurt by technological changes such as automation and by the economic competition from minority groups. Most were socially isolated in their communities, had few friends and poor communication with their families. Most refused to express any remorse over their actions.

THE NEO-NAZIS

In general the researchers concluded that the neo-Nazi youths lacked poise and had a sense of "insecurity and inadequacy." They were socially isolated and psychologically weak; their school performance was poor; and their family life was unstable. Evidently, the young Nazis found security in the neo-Nazi ideology. It gave them a group to belong to, and it stressed primitive concepts of masculinity and power. According to author Martin Deutsch, "For many of these youths, the militarism, the paraphernalia, the organized purposes of neo-Nazism probably can be reduced to the need to identify with organized fear-instilling power. For others, it might operate on the unconscious level as a compensation for their own feelings of isolation and inadequacy."

We began this chapter by asking the question, What kind of person becomes a Nazi? The answer depends on prevailing social and historical conditions that favor or disfavor the movement. It also depends on the personality of the people involved. Under today's conditions, Nazism seems to attract individuals with serious social and psychological problems who find solace in a bizarre group life that provides theoretical justification for antisocial attitudes and even violence.

10
FREE SPEECH FOR NAZIS?

> Congress shall make no law respecting an establishment of religion, or prohibiting the free exercise thereof; or abridging the freedom of speech, or of the press; or the right of the people peaceably to assemble, and to petition the government for a redress of grievances.—First Amendment to the Constitution of the United States

> We reject the notion that the advocacy of genocide by individuals or groups such as the American Nazi Party, and, particularly demonstrations such as they are planning for Skokie are entitled to First Amendment protection of the freedom of speech which is one of the blessings of American Democracy. —Central Conference of American Rabbis

Frank Collin was thrown out of the American Nazi Party in 1970 when his Nazi comrades

THE NEO-NAZIS

learned that he was the son of a Jewish victim of the Holocaust, a survivor of the Dachau concentration camp. Collin refused to give up on Nazism, however. He set up the National Socialist Party of America (NSPA), which is based in Chicago. Under Collin's leadership, the NSPA never consisted of more than a couple dozen young troublemakers, racist thugs without much influence. But beginning in February 1977 and lasting for a period of fourteen months, Collin transformed himself and his ragtag collection of followers into front-page news.

It all started when Collin applied for permission to stage a Nazi rally in Skokie, Illinois, a suburb of Chicago. A heated controversy ensued. Was the proposed Nazi rally protected by the First Amendment guarantees of freedom of speech, the press, and assembly? The free-speech issue and the political insignificance of the NSPA were obscured in the emotional furor that surrounded the rally. Many critics likened Collin to Hitler and his storm troopers. In reality, however, Collin and the NSPA members resembled their idols only in their wildest dreams and fantasies. The episode gave the NSPA and neo-Nazism more media attention than they ever would have gotten if the handful of party stalwarts had been allowed to show up at Skokie Town Hall and display their "Free Speech for Whites" posters for one hour, as originally planned.

By 1980, Collin was out of the limelight—and out of the Nazi organization—following his arrest and imprisonment on morals charges. Collin may be gone, but the free-speech issue he raised, and took

Free Speech for Nazis?

Anti-Nazi protesters in Chicago's Marquette Park in 1978. Two thousand people took part in the peaceful demonstration.

advantage of to capture media attention, still remains.

It is doubtful that Frank Collin ever really wanted to demonstrate in Skokie. In 1977 he was in the middle of litigation filed against the city of Chicago by the American Civil Liberties Union (ACLU) on his behalf. This lawsuit sought to overturn an exorbitant insurance bond demanded by the city for permission for the Nazis to continue their rallies in Chicago's Marquette Park. The ACLU believes that the civil liberties of even the most unpopular political groups and individuals must be protected under the First Amendment, as a guarantee of freedom for everyone. The ACLU may not always agree with their clients, but they will defend their right of free speech. The ACLU contested the insurance requirement as a subterfuge meant to deny Collin his right to free speech.

The litigation looked as if it might drag on for months or even years. This was very distressing to Collin and his followers, for whom publicity and attention are about the only benefits that accrue from NSPA membership. Collin sent letters to local leaders in a dozen or more Chicago suburbs requesting permission to stage a rally in town parks. Most of the suburban leaders simply ignored the letters. But officials in Skokie responded by insisting on even higher insurance bond requirements than Chicago had asked for. The Nazis responded by announcing plans for a one-hour protest demonstration by thirty party members on the sidewalk outside Skokie Town Hall. They would use no loudspeaker and would not march in the street. They would carry signs that called for free speech for Nazis.

Skokie officials were alarmed. The village has a large Jewish population that includes seven thousand Holocaust survivors. A Nazi demonstration in such a town would be very provocative. At first officials asked local clergymen to persuade residents to ignore the demonstration, but this plan collapsed when angry Holocaust survivors denounced the demonstration and reminded people of the Nazi atrocities in the death camps.

The issue was no longer Frank Collins and his tiny band of misfits, but Hitler and his storm troopers and death camps. Tolerance for the neo-Nazis'

Free Speech for Nazis?

rights under the Constitution was equated with condoning genocide. Fearing violence, village officials obtained a court injunction blocking the demonstration. They also drafted a series of local ordinances demanding exorbitant insurance and requiring thirty days' notice before holding any public demonstration. In addition to this, they banned the display of materials considered offensive to the community and the wearing of military-style uniforms in demonstrations. They also prohibited the distribution of literature that contained "group libel." These ordinances were obviously designed to ban Nazis from ever demonstrating in Skokie.

The ground was set for a classic free-speech fight. Everyone but Collin and his entourage agreed that the Nazis' political message was immoral, bigoted, and obnoxious, but were they entitled to the guarantees of free speech, free press, and free assembly promised by the First Amendment to the Constitution? A number of key arguments against allowing the Nazis to demonstrate were developed both in courtroom litigation and in public debate over this issue. These main arguments can be summarized as follows:

1. *Nazis don't deserve First Amendment protection.* The Nazis forfeited their claim to First Amendment rights by advocating the destruction of the basic values and freedoms of a democratic society. If they were to win support for their views and get elected to power, they would destroy our democratic system. When

the Founding Fathers wrote the First Amendment, they intended it as a guarantee that democracy would thrive, not as a license for those who would destroy freedom.

2. *Mental anguish.* Permitting the Nazis to demonstrate in Skokie, bearing swastikas and wearing Nazi uniforms, would cause mental anguish to the thousands of survivors of the concentration camps who live in that community. Some people called this "menticide."

3. *Incitement to riot and hecklers' veto.* The Nazi demonstration would inevitably incite violence and disorder because of the deep-seated anti-Nazi feelings in the community and the anger the Nazis would provoke. The government is responsible for maintaining law and order, and could block the demonstration from occurring. This argument is called "hecklers' veto" because it gives hecklers the right to veto the demonstration.

4. *Group libel.* The First Amendment should not protect "group libel," which includes insults, slurs, and denunciations of an entire ethnic group. Under this argument the First Amendment would not protect anti-black or anti-Semitic speech or literature.

5. *Fighting words.* The use of "fighting words," such as anti-Semitic insults and the display of Nazi symbols, which might provoke a fight, is not protected by the First Amendment and can be banned.

The response to all these arguments by civil libertarians was quite simple: not one of them is valid.

Free Speech for Nazis?

The main counterarguments can be summarized as follows:

1. *Nazis don't deserve freedom of speech.* The Supreme Court has always held that freedom of speech and of the press is guaranteed to all citizens regardless of how reprehensible their views. Time and time again the courts have ruled that the "expression of racist and anti-Semitic views in a public place and the right to assemble in a public place for the purpose of communicating and discussing racist and anti-Semitic views" are protected by the Constitution. The editors of *America,* a lay Catholic journal summed up the counterargument this way: "in our society the choice has been made that, with respect to peaceful demonstrations, the legal right to demonstrate shall not depend upon the justice or the morality of the demonstrators' cause." Civil libertarians argue that the real test of freedom is society's ability to tolerate the expression of unpopular ideas. They often cite the words of Chief Justice Oliver Wendell Holmes, who spoke of the "principle of free thought—not free thought for those who agree with us but freedom for the thought we hate."

2. *Mental anguish.* The overriding necessity to protect freedom of speech and assembly takes precedence over any mental anguish an observer might suffer. In any case, no one was forced to view the demonstration, which was planned not as a march through residential streets but as a demonstration at Town Hall. If the display of Nazi symbols were banned be-

cause of the potential mental anguish it might cause, movies and television dramas featuring such symbols would also have to be banned.
3. *Incitement to riot and hecklers' veto.* The crime known as *incitement to riot* does not include speeches that trigger a riotous reaction by the audience. It applies only to a speaker who calls listeners to take illegal, violent action and succeeds in convincing them to do so. Incitement to riot is punishable only *after* it has happened. In other words, a speaker who incites a crowd to riot can be arrested only *after* he has done so. He cannot be blocked from speaking in advance. If a demonstration could be prohibited because it advocates unpopular ideas and would likely provoke a violent response by opponents, then Martin Luther King, Jr., would never have been allowed to march from Selma to Montgomery in 1965 or to march for integrated housing in Cicero, a white Chicago suburb, in 1966, and the anti–Vietnam War movement would never have gotten off the ground. If majority hecklers are allowed to veto the exercise of free speech by unpopular minorities then only the expression of majority views will be safe, and freedom will be jeopardized.
4. *Group libel.* Court rulings have consistently upheld the right to freedom of expression of political views regardless of how insulting they might be to any particular segment of the population.
5. *Fighting words.* This doctrine had never before been applied to symbols such as swastikas. Nor had it been used as an argument for prior

> restraint of speech. Former ACLU member David Hamlin argues that the "fighting words" doctrine is generally used after the fact in "one-on-one confrontations (typically, when a demonstrator called a policeman something which evoked a physical response instantly)."

Despite the public uproar and the hesitation of local courts, there was really very little doubt about the final outcome of the Skokie case. Federal courts eventually upheld the ACLU arguments and overturned all the restrictions against the Nazis' exercise of free speech. The Nazis were free to stage their demonstration in Skokie. In his ruling U.S. District Court Judge Bernard Decker wrote, "It must be made clear from the outset that defendants [Skokie] have no power to prevent plaintiffs [Collin] from stating their opinions of black and Jewish people, however noxious and reprehensible that philosophy may be. The Supreme Court has held that 'above all else, the First Amendment means that government has no power to restrict expression because of its message, its ideas, its subject matter, or its content.' "

Ironically, Collin and the NSPA never exercised their hard-won right to demonstrate in Skokie. They primarily wanted publicity and attention, so that they might continue to appeal to the minuscule audience of white racists who were open to their ideas in the South Chicago area around Marquette Park. By the time their legal victory was achieved, it was clear that to go ahead with their demonstration in Skokie would provoke a huge counterdemonstration, not only by local Jews and others in Skokie, but also by a wide-ranging coalition of anti-fascists, leftists, and Jews from around the country. The threat of a violent confrontation, which the outnumbered Nazis would be sure to lose, was very real. Instead of going to Skokie, Collin settled for a twenty-minute demonstration in Federal Plaza in Chicago. For security reasons two dozen NSPA members were driven in a police van to the Federal Building for their rally. Several thousand angry counterdemonstrators shouted their indignation and drowned out Collin's speech, as police tried to keep the rival factions separated.

The case of Frank Collin and the NSPA is now history, and the right of free speech for all, including Nazis, has the full force of law in our land. But there are issues here that we will have to think about for the future. In our country, refusing to serve a person at a lunch counter because of his or her religion or race is considered an affront to human dignity and is against the law. But to advocate genocide against a group of people because of the color of their skin or their religion is a legal exercise of free speech. It seems paradoxical. In Skokie, the Nazis' freedom of speech, press, and assembly were decided in a uniquely American context, under the guidelines of the Constitution, the Bill of Rights, and Supreme Court rulings interpreting those documents. But the arguments put forth by civil libertarians were couched in universal themes. The argument was made repeatedly, for

Free Speech for Nazis?

example, that the test of any democracy is the tolerance of expressions of unpopular or even despicable ideas. There is no denial that democratic values have an international scope. Nazism, too, is an international phenomenon. It is certainly relevant for us to examine how the world of democratic community has dealt with the question of reconciling a commitment to democratic ideals with the advocacy of racism and genocide by neo-Nazi and other fascist organizations. Is freedom really jeopardized if the advocacy of racism and genocide is prohibited? This serious question was at the heart of the Skokie debate.

Several other democratic nations see no problem in banning the expression of such views and simultaneously maintaining a democratic society. Several countries that have endured fascist rule have denied such groups full democratic rights. In West Germany, for example, the distribution of certain types of fascist and Nazi literature is punishable by up to three years' imprisonment. The political activities of fascist groups are restricted in Italy, and Portugal has an anti-fascist law that imposes an eight-year prison sentence on violators. Norway limits the distribution of neo-Nazi literature. Other countries prohibit the expression of racism. In New Zealand it is an offense to encourage race discrimination. In the Netherlands it is against the law to infringe on the rights of others. In Sweden, "discrimination against or contempt of ethnic groups" can be punished by up to two years in jail. In Ireland there are restrictions on groups that advocate violence. In England, the Race Relations Act of

1965 restricts the publication and distribution of racist literature. All of these countries are Western democracies in which citizens enjoy individual freedom and political rights. Indeed, five of them—New Zealand, the Netherlands, Norway, Sweden, and Great Britain—received a higher human rights rating in Charles Humana's *World Human Rights Guide* than did the United States.

Free speech for Nazis is not a simple issue, and it will not disappear easily.

As long as the neo-Nazis exist, the issue of their right to spread their poison in our democratic society will be raised again and again. As we can see, other democracies have dealt with the issue in different ways.

11
THE THREAT OF NAZISM TODAY

Unfortunately history has not closed the book on Nazism. The Nazi empire was destroyed in World War II. The racist and totalitarian dreams of Adolf Hitler and his followers were discredited. Nazi war criminals were tried and punished. But still the poisonous ideology of hatred, racism, and authoritarianism somehow survives. It provides a forum for old fascist veterans who refuse to give up the faded dreams, and it attracts new adherents.

How dangerous are the neo-Nazis? Experts sometimes differ in their assessment of the neo-Nazi threat, but some things are very clear. The neo-Nazi movement has a different impact in different countries, largely depending on specific historical circumstances. The appeal of neo-Nazi groups in countries such as Spain or Germany, which have had a strong fascist tradition, is different than it is in the United States, Britain, or Scandinavia. But even in those nations where neo-Nazism has its greatest presence, it is extremely weak. It is a small minority movement existing on the fringes of political life. The social, economic, and political conditions that favored fascism do not exist today. Now it is only the hard-core extremist, the authoritarian-personality types, who are attracted to neo-Nazism. Their ideology, their paraphernalia, and their activities find very little favor in society as a whole. There is not much danger that a Nazi party will win mass political support and take power, through elections or a coup d'état, in any major industrial nation.

Some developing countries have been or continue to be ruled by right-wing military dictators. Although these regimes are sometimes described as fascist, they are not identical with the mass fascist movements based in the socially and economically dislocated middle classes of the 1930s. In developing countries, the recent trend has been toward relaxation of military rule and the reinstitution of democratic procedures, as in Argentina and Bolivia. In those nations where the process of democratization is not yet complete, democratic mass movements are on the rise, as in Chile and the Philippines. Nazi rule is nowhere to be seen on the political horizon.

The political impotence of Nazism is especially apparent in the United States. According to a report issued by the Anti-Defamation League in the late 1970s, the American neo-Nazi movement "remains a mixed gang of young malcontents and mis-

The Threat of Nazism Today

fits, older hatemongers and other contorted personalities, whose visibility is altogether disproportionate to their small numbers." In an interview in 1984, Jerome Bakst, director of ADL research, said that American neo-Nazis do "not pose any threat to the U.S. Republic. The Ku Klux Klan is a greater danger because it has roots in native America. The Nazis have a foreign flavor." Bakst contrasted the Nazi movement in the thirties with the neo-Nazi movement of today: "The American Nazi movement in the thirties was an extension of the movement in Germany." But this is not so today. In Bakst's view the American "neo-Nazis don't have much of a future."

This does not mean that neo-Nazism is not dangerous. The people who are attracted to this movement are often unstable, disturbed, violent, and dangerous. Nazi philosophy gives political and moral validity to their deep-seated hatred of blacks and Jews, and justifies antisocial behavior. The Nazi ideology classifies "non-Aryans" as subhuman and sees them as the incarnation of evil. This makes it very easy for neo-Nazis to rationalize violence against them. The potential consequences of this ideology of hatred came to light recently in media accounts of criminal investigations of the Aryan Nations in Idaho. NBC-TV News broadcast videotapes of Aryan Nations leader Richard Butler preaching to his followers. Butler said "Hate the evil, you are told by Scripture. Hate with a perfect hatred. Hate it with every fiber of your being. Hate is our law." Former members of the Aryan Nations have been charged with a number of bank and armored car robberies in the West. They have also been accused of having murdered Alan Berg, a radio commentator in Denver, who was Jewish. Keith Gilbert, an ex-convict who was recruited to neo-Nazism while in prison, told NBC News that the goal of the movement is to establish "a national homeland for our people. Anything in furtherance of this holy cause is approved without exception." Asked if this included violence, Gilbert responded, "Violence or whatever."

The danger posed by neo-Nazism lies not in its political potential, but its potential for terrorism and violence. The American Federation of Labor and Congress of Industrial Organizations assessed the Nazi threat in these terms: "The danger of American Nazism . . . is not that it has the capacity to engulf America or capture our government and its institutions. Rather, the concern is and should be with its harmful effects on emotionally unstable or zealous adherents."

The neo-Nazis' long list of violent acts, their fascination with guns, and their criminal records underscore this danger. A number of Jewish and liberal organizations, including the Anti-Defamation League and the Simon Wiesenthal Center in Los Angeles, have concentrated efforts on keeping track of neo-Nazis organizations and their members and exposing their activities. Recently law-enforcement agencies have taken a growing interest in criminal activities traceable to neo-Nazi organizations and their current and former members.

The First Amendment may guarantee the neo-Nazis the freedom to express their hatred, but no law protects their violence. Democratic society may have to tolerate their political pronouncements, but not their terrorist attacks. By their own actions, the neo-Nazis may someday provoke the suppression of neo-Nazism in America.

BIBLIOGRAPHY

BOOKS AND PAMPHLETS

Adorno, T. W.; Frankel-Brunswik, Else; Levinson, Daniel J.; and Sanford, R. Nevitt. *The Authoritarian Personality.* Abridged Ed. New York: Norton, 1982.

American Jewish Committee. *Policy Statement Re: Response to Neo-Nazis in the United States.* New York: March 21, 1978.

Anti-Defamation League of B'Nai B'Rith. *Extremism on the Right.* New York: B'Nai B'Rith, 1983.

Anti-Defamation League of B'Nai B'Rith. *Hate Groups in America: A Record of Bigotry and Violence.* New York: B'Nai B'Rith, n.d.

Anti-Defamation League of B'Nai B'Rith. *Terrorism's Targets: Democracy, Israel and Jews.* New York: B'Nai B'Rith, 1981.

Billig, Michael. *Fascism: A Social Psychological View of the National Front.* New York: Academic Press, 1978.

Central Conference of American Rabbis. Press Release. April 5, 1978.

Compton, James V. *The Swastika and the Eagle.* Boston: Houghton Mifflin, 1967.

BIBLIOGRAPHY

Diamond, Sander A. *The Nazi Movement in the United States, 1924–1941.* Ithaca, N.Y.: Cornell University Press, 1974.

Ellerin, Milton. *American Nazis: Myth or Menace?* New York: American Jewish Committee, November 22, 1977.

Frye, Alton. *Nazi German and the American Hemisphere, 1933–1941.* New Haven, Conn.: Yale University Press, 1983.

Grolnick, William A. "Skokie and Beyond." (pamphlet) American Jewish Committee, April 1, 1978.

Hamlin, David. *The Nazi-Skokie Conflict: A Civil Liberties Battle.* Boston: Beacon Press, 1980.

Hickory, William Ernest. *Freedom of the Press.* Chicago: University of Chicago Press, 1947.

Katz, William Loren. *An Album of Nazism.* New York: Franklin Watts, 1979.

McKale, Donald M. *The Swastika Outside Germany.* Kent, Ohio: Kent State University Press, 1977.

Rogge, John O. *Official German Report.* New York: T. Yossler, 1961.

Sterling, Claire. *The Terror Network.* New York: Holt, Rinehart & Winston, 1981.

Walkman, Ernest. *A Legacy of Hate: Anti-Semitism in America.* New York: Franklin Watts, 1982.

NEO-NAZI PUBLICATIONS:

Defiance: Voice of White America, National Socialist Liberation Front.
The National Socialist, World Union of National Socialists.

National Socialist League, National Socialist League.
National Vanguard, National Alliance.
Stormer, National Socialist White Workers Party.

ARTICLES

AFL-CIO. "American Nazism—Myth or Menace." *American Federationist,* March 1978.

Arkes, Hadline. "Marching through Skokie." *National Review,* May 12, 1978.

Barr, Albert. "Of Attempts to Disprove the Holocaust." *New York Times,* February 16, 1977.

Berman, Paul L. "Crackpot History and the Right to Lie." *Village Voice,* June 16, 1981.

"Cleveland: Nazi Killer Is Sentenced to Death." *Newsweek,* August 22, 1983.

Coleman, Daniel. "Anti-Semitism: A Prejudice That Takes Many Guises." *New York Times,* September 4, 1984.

Deutsch, Martin. "The 1960 Swastika Smearings: An Evaluation of the Apprehended Youth." *Merrill-Palmer Quarterly,* 1962.

Dawidowicz, Lucy S. "Lies about the Holocaust." *Commentary,* December 1980.

"Even for Nazis." *The Progressive,* December 1977.

"Friends of the New Germany: The Bund . . ." *Journal of Modern History,* 1957.

Haley, Alex. "Interview with George Lincoln Rockwell." *Playboy,* April 1966.

BIBLIOGRAPHY

Hentoff, Nat. "First Amendment Watch: Summer Soldiers of the First Amendment ." *Inquiry,* March 20, 1978.

"Hitler Heirs in the U.S.A." *Patterns of Prejudice,* September–October 1977.

King, Seth S. "Professor Causes Furor by Saying Nazi Slaying of Jews Is a Myth." *New York Times,* January 28, 1977.

Lake, Peter. "Inside the American Nazi Party." *The Rebel,* three-part series beginning January 30, 1984.

Lewin, Isaac. "Of Nazis, Jews and Professor Butz's Painstaking Research." (Letters to the Editor) *New York Times,* February 4. 1977.

Lindsey, Robert. "Auschwitz Survivor Sues Institute of Historical Review." *New York Times,* March 6, 1981.

Mathews, Tom. "The Nazi of New Rochelle." *Newsweek,* February 28, 1977.

Mill, Jonathan. "The Making of a Nazi: Frank Collin's Roots." *New Republic,* July 1, 1978.

"Nazis in Skokie, The." *America,* June 17, 1978.

"Revising Holocaust History." *Christian Century,* July 16–23, 1980.

Robinove, Samuel. "Skokie and the First Amendment." *Keeping Posted,* February 1979.

Rosen, A. Abbot. "Hatred on the March." *Anti-Defamation League Bulletin,* 1977.

"Thoughts about Skokie." *Dissent,* Spring 1979.

Will, George F. "Nazis: Outside the Constitution." *Washington Post,* February 2, 1978.

Wolf, Gerard R. "Of Nazis, Jews and Professor Butz's Painstaking Research." (Letters to the Editor) *New York Times,* February 4, 1977.

INDEX

Allen, Michael, 72
American Mercury (magazine), 49
Anti-Defamation League, 114; Liberty Lobby suit against, 50; tracking of Neo-Nazi organizations, 148
Anti-Semitism, influence of early childhood experiences in developing, 129–130; propaganda, 120–122; roots in Europe, 19–20
Arnoud, Francois, 115–116
Aryan Nations (organization), 83–87
Aryan race, 18–19
Authoritarian personality, description, 128–129

Barnes, Harry Elmer, 47–48
Billig, Michael, 112
Black International (organization), 114–115
"Blasting the Historical Blackout" (Barnes), 47
Brannen, Robert, 78–79
British National Front, 111–113
Bund der Freunde des Neuven Deutschland (Friends of the New Germany), 29–30; membership in America, 34, 37
Butler, Richard, 119
Butz, Arthur R., 51–53

Carlson, Gerald R., 96
Carto, Willis, Liberty Lobby and, 48–51
  National Alliance and, 80–81; pro-Nazi writings, 49; visit of Yockey in prison, 44–45
Collin, Frank, 69, 71–72, 133–143
Covington, Harold, 72

Dawidowicz, Lucy S., 45–47, 53–54
Debbaudt, Jean Roberts, 110, 115
Defiance (newspaper), 75
Deutschtum (concept), 29
Dietz, George, 118
Drama of the European Jews, The (Rassinier), 45, 48

Ellerin, Milton, 63
Erickson, Bert, 109

INDEX

Erlanger, Alexi, 118, 119
European Liberation Front (organization), 44
European New Order. *See* Black International (organization)

Fascism, absolute control of mass media, 12; anti-capitalist orientation, 12; compared with Nazism, 12; compared with totalitarianism, 11–12; defined, 11; garrison-state mentality, 13; police state tactics, 13; social conditions favoring, 127; suppression of civil liberties, 12; suppression of labor unions, 12
Faurisson, Robert, 53
First Amendment, of the U.S. Constitution, guarantees, 133–139, 141
Ford Motor Company, and the Teutonia Association, 25
Franco, Francisco (General), 108
Freedom of speech controversy, for Neo-Nazis, 133–144; First Amendment protection, 137, 139; group libel, 138, 140; incitement to riot and hecklers' veto argument, 138, 140; "mental anguish" argument, 138, 139; restriction in other countries, 143, 144; Skokie controversy, 134–137; Supreme court rulings, 139; use of fighting words, 138, 140
Freikorps (groups), 15
Friends of the New Germany (organization), 29, 34, 37
Fuerza Nueva (Spain), 108

Garrison-state mentality, 13
Gauleitung USA (organization), 25–26
Genocide, 43, 60–61, advocacy of, 133
German immigration to the U.S., 23–24
Gissibl, Friedrich Fritz, 24
Griebl, Ignatz, 32

Hand, Karl, Jr., 75–76
Hess, Rudolf, 16, 29, 30, 101–102
Hinckley, John W., Jr., 72
Hitler, Adolf, early childhood experiences, 125; fanatical hatred of Jews, 19, 18–21, 125; founding of Nazism, 13–14; imprisonment, 15–16; *Mein Kampf,* 16, 19, 21, 57, 118, 125; organization of Nazi Party, 15; skillful manipulation of people, 125
Hoax of the Twentieth Century, The (Butz), 51–53
Hoggan, David L., 46–47
Holocaust, 43–44; revisionism, 46–54

Imperium (Yockey), 44
Inflation, Germany in the 1920s, 16, 17
Institute for Historical Review, 51
International cooperation, of Neo-Nazis, 114–122; coordination and distribution of propaganda, 114; coordination of terrorism, 114, 116; exchange of information, 114, 118; joint military training, 117; sponsorship of annual festivities, 116; support of radical groups, 115
International propaganda, anti-Semitic literature, 120–122

Kamaradenwerk, 117, 118
Kasper, John, 64

Index

Koehl, Matt, 64–67
Krausnick, Helmut, 46
Kuhn, Fritz, 25, 34–39
Ku Klux Klan, 71

Lake, Peter, 130–131
Lauck, Gary Rex, 73–74
League of St. George (Great Britain), 111–113
Lewin, Isaac, 52
Liberation Movement of the German Reich (organization), 101
Liberty Bell Publications, 82–83
Liberty Lobby (organization), 48–50
Lynch, Connie (Reverend), 89–92

Mein Kampf (Hitler), 16, 19, 21, 57, 118, 125
"Melting pot" theory, 28
Mengele, Josef, 117
Milam, Dennis, 72

National Alliance, 80–82
National Renaissance Party, 64
National Socialist German Workers Party, 11; overseas organization, 27–28, 73
National Socialist League, 76–78
National Socialist Liberation Front, 74–76
National Socialist Mobilizer (newspaper), 77
National Socialist Movement, 78–79
National Socialist Party of America (NSPA), 69, 134, 136, 141–142; electoral participation, 94–95
National Socialist White Workers Party, 74
National Socialist White People's Party (NSWPP) 64, 67, 69, 96
National Socialist World (magazine), 81
National States Rights Party, 64, 88–89; anti-black violence support, 90; attacks against Jews, 91; developing international links, 119–120
Nazi Party. *See* National Socialist German Workers Party
Nazism, atrocities, 43–44; coordination of terrorism, 116–118; German-American attitude towards, 31–32, 33; German form of fascism, 13; international links, 114–122; international propaganda, 120–122; mass manipulation in, 19; *Mein Kampf*, ideological basis for, 16–17; Palestine Liberation Organization and, 115–116, 122; potential for terrorism and violence, 148; psychology of, 123–132; revival after the war, 44–46; revisionism, 46–48; Social Darwinism and, 17–18; threat to society, assessment of, 145–149
Nazism, in America, 22–41; American Nazi Party, 55, 68; failure of penetration, 39–41; formation in New York, 22, 24; Gauleitung USA and, 25, 26; German-American attitudes towards, 32, 33; growth of movement, 22; Rockwell (George Lincoln), role in, 55–64; Teutonia Association, role in, 24–26
Nazism, in Belgium, 109–110
Nazism, in France, 106–108

INDEX

Nazism, in Great Britain, 111–113
Nazism, in Italy, 104–106; terrorism by rightist elements, 104–105
Nazism, in Spain, 108–109
Nazism, in Sweden, 111
Nazism, in West Germany, organization and membership, 99–100
Neo-Nazism. *See* Nazism
Nordiske Rikspartiet (Sweden), 111
Nuremberg trials, 43–44

Oredsson, Goran Assar, 111
Origins and Originators of World War II (Hoggan), 46–47
Origins of World War II (Taylor), 45–46

Palestine Liberation Organization, support of Neo-Nazis, 115, 116, 122
Patler, John, 64
Pearson, Drew, 50
Pierce, William L., 81
Prejudicial attitudes, influence of early childhood experiences on, 129
Protocols of the Elders of Zion, The, 118, 121–122
Psychology, of Nazism, 123–132; authoritarian personality, 128–129; bandwagon effect, 127; boundless thirst for absolute power, 125; expression of repressed sexuality, 125; fanatical hatred of Jews, 125; fascination for Nazi memorabilia and guns, 131; influence of early childhood experiences, 129; insecurity and inadequacy of self, 132; insecurity of individual freedom, 126; mass manipulation, 125; need to identify with organized fear-instilling power, 132; opportunism, 127; paranoia as overriding emotion, 130; racial unconsciousness, 125; social avoidance of ostracism, 127; social isolation, 131; troublemakers at school, 131; underachievers in school, 131
Putsch (uprising), 15, 30

Qaddafi, Muammar el-, 115

Rassinier, Paul, 45, 48
"Revisionism: A Key to Peace" (Barnes), 48
Rockwell, George Lincoln, 55–63; anti-Semitism, 56–57; assassination, 55, 64; attitude toward genocide, 60; early interaction with Jews, 56; early life, 56; enlistment in the military, 57; founding of Nazi Party, 55; involvement with right-wing politics, 57; racist views, 59–60
Roeder, Manfred, 87, 101, 102–104; international neo-Nazi network, role in, 117–119
Rust, David C., 75

Schnurch, Hubert, 32
Schuster, Josef, 24, 30
Security Services Action Group, 79–80
Signorelli, Paolo, 105
Skokie (Illinois), Nazi rally controversy in, 134–142
Social Darwinism, 17–18
Spanish Circle of Friends of Europe (Cedade), 109
Spanknobel, Heinz, 29–32
Spearhead, The (magazine), 113

Index

Spotlight, The (newspaper), 49
Sterling, Claire, 110, 114
Stoner, J. B., 88–89, 91–92; electoral campaigns, 93–94

Taylor, A. J., 45–46
Terror Network, The (Sterling), 110
Teutonia Association, 24, 25, 26; membership in Detroit, 25
Teutonic Unity (newsletter), 103
This Time the World (Rockwell), 59
Thunderbolt (newspaper), 92, 93
Tomassi, Joseph, National Socialist Liberation Front and, 74–75
Totalitarianism, 11–12

Treaty of Versailles, 15
Tyndall, John, 112, 120

United German Societies, 31; Nazi attempts to take over, 32; withdrawal of Jewish organizations from, 32

Veh, Robert, 77–78
Vincent, Allen, 74
Vlaamese Militanten Orde (Belgium), 109–110
Vogel, Hans Jochen, 100

Weimar Republic, 15
World Union of National Socialists (organization), 61

Yockey, Francis Parker, 44, 45

ABOUT THE AUTHOR

JERRY BORNSTEIN is a graduate of New York University. While working as a freelance writer he had a number of articles published in newspapers and magazines. He is the author of *Unions in Transition,* and with his wife Sandy, he wrote *What Is Genetics?* and *New Frontiers in Genetics.* Mr. Bornstein works as a news researcher for a television network in New York City.